THE
PROBLEM
WITH BEING
A PERSON

THE PROBLEM WITH BEING A PERSON

. . . .

How an Existentialish Philosophy Can
Ground Us in Modern Chaos

TALIA POLLOCK

Tarcher
an imprint of Penguin Random House
New York

Tarcher

an imprint of Penguin Random House LLC
1745 Broadway, New York, NY 10019
penguinrandomhouse.com

Book design by Angie Boutin

Library of Congress Cataloging-in-Publication Data has been applied for.
Hardcover ISBN: 9780593420904
Ebook ISBN: 9780593420911

Printed in the United States of America
1st Printing

The authorized representative in the EU for product safety and compliance is
Penguin Random House Ireland, Morrison Chambers, 32 Nassau Street,
Dublin D02 YH68, Ireland, https://eu-contact.penguin.ie.

For and because of Hannah.
You are meaning out the wazoo.

CONTENTS

. . . .

THE
PROBLEM
WITH BEING
A PERSON

Preface: Red Light, Green Light

· · · · · · · · · · · ·

I wash down a mouthful of sugar cookie crumbs with a gulp of cold lemonade fresh from a pack of powder. Then I stand, toss my Dixie cup into the overflowing trash bin encircled by a large family of bees, and jog over to the field. I can hear the lemonade sloshing in my stomach, and I can feel butterflies in there, too, drowning in tidal waves of pink sugar water.

"All right, guys!" the sixteen-year-old counselor calls out. "Take your places."

All thirty of us campers line up on a white spray-painted line on the grassy field.

I size up my opponents, all four feet of them. Long legs—fast. Sports goggles—cerebral. Jumping up and down—enthusiastic today but anointed ADHD in ten years and dependent on Ritalin in fifteen.

"You all remember the rules of the game, right?" the boy in charge asks. "When I say 'green light,' you move. When I say 'red light,' you freeze. If I catch you moving even a smidge after

I said 'red light,' you have to go back to the start. The first one to tag me wins."

A symphony of hoots and hollers breaks out. One kid's voice pierces the choir as he shouts, "What does the winner get?!"

"You get to be It," says the counselor. "Which means you get to tell everyone else what to do!"

The hoots and hollers return as the counselor walks twenty feet away from the group. He plants himself with power and shouts, "Green light!"

We run around while the counselor shouts colors at random. At every "red light," at least a couple of campers fail to freeze in time and get shipped back to the start, their progress negated, enthusiasm extinguished over that one uncontrolled twitch. But with every "green light," the collective optimism kicks back into high gear.

Whenever I think back to this childhood game, I feel an inner sense of chaos. I remember the pandemonium of motion, the apprehension of not knowing which color was coming next, the erratic movements that would've surely led to an ACL tear if any of us had weighed over ninety pounds.

I can recall my powerlessness, my acceleration, and my deceleration commanded by a teen with too much power.

For me, it's effortless to jump back into the anxious feeling of Red Light, Green Light, because I still play it today. Except instead of a bellowing "green light," I hear *You're enough!* And in place of "red light," it's *You're made for more!* And instead of being managed by a high schooler getting paid $12 an hour, I'm being conducted by society.

Educators believe Red Light, Green Light is a great game because it trains kids to listen with concentration and respond with control and intention. It also has built-in cardio! And an invaluable life lesson! While it may seem at first that winning is a by-product of being strong and nimble, we quickly learn that it's in fact the best *listeners* who are the victorious ones. (And the most obedient.)

We're taught that the champion is the one who's the strongest at complying. So, later in life, when the person who is It tells us that we'll be happy when we have a consistent morning routine, a side-hustle-turned-job you love so much that work doesn't even feel like work, or full eyebrows even though yesterday's It banned brows thicker than a No. 2 pencil, we apply our well-honed listening skills from summer camp—and comply.

> *Listen to your body!*
> *You never regret a workout.*
> *Imagine where you could be next year if you start now.*
> *Live in the moment, because it's all you've got.*
> *Your career doesn't define you.*
> *You are what you do.*
> *Be yourself!*
> *Fake it till you make it.*
> *Good things come to those who hustle.*
> *SELF-CARE!*
> *You can sleep when you're dead.*
> *SELF-CARE!*
> *Follow your gut.*
> *Follow this fail-proof system.*

We are fed such contradicting instructions, at such a rapid pace, that most of us survive by idling in "yellow light." Otherwise, the whiplash is too strenuous—it's likely what keeps 78 percent of chiropractors in business.

Whether the topic is happiness, beauty, success, meaning, or purpose, every commandment has a counter-commandment.

It's comical, really. Absurd, some might say.

It used to be that receiving all this conflicting advice was at least an intentional pursuit. Attending a seminar, buying a book, listening to Dr. Laura Schlessinger on the radio or Dr. Phil on the TV, glancing up in a high school gym locker room. But now we get red-lighted, green-lighted even with—especially with—our heads down. Memes, clips, magazine ads, TV commercials, even the sidewalk board at the bar down the street has an instruction for how to live.

It's no wonder the games of Red Light, Green Light would quickly dismantle: the girls got bored and formed clusters; the boys took water breaks; the counselor who was almighty at the beginning lost steam.

I remember standing on the field with my eyes wide and my head ping-ponging back and forth. I remember floating out of my body to get an overhead view of my options. I remember not knowing if I should be giving it all my effort like those sweaty, breathless boys, or if I should opt out and stand in the huddle of whispering girls. I remember knowing that the point was to *want* to be It, but that desire had no appeal. And that concerned me. I remember that concern turning to shame—what was *wrong with me* for not wanting to win the game? I remember questioning: If winning is not the point of my existence, well then, what is?

And then I heard the counselor blow his whistle and say, "Game over, guys!" and I felt relieved to not have to think about this again until tomorrow.

1

Normal°

We were going on hour three of our Zoom hypnobirthing class when Cynthia explained that a relaxed throat equals a relaxed vagina.

"Once you've reached ten centimeters of dilation," she said, "you should start deep breathing through your nose all the way to the lower back of your throat and down through your body behind baby." I closed my eyes to practice visualizing my baby gliding out of me like a kid on the blue tarp of a slip-and-slide positioned perfectly on a bright green grassy backyard hill.

It must have been the image of our daughter's ejection out of me that had ejected Jesse off the couch, down the hall, and into my office, which we had begun converting into our nursery, with a tape measure in tow. When the virtual birthing class ended, I headed for bed to listen to my peaceful-delivery mantras and visualize my relaxed vagina as I fell into a deep slumber. As I passed by him, I caught a glimpse of Jesse maniacally taking measurements.

The next morning, we rendezvoused at the kitchen table, where he, straight-faced like he was presenting possible solutions to the very distressing beaver overpopulation problem continually brought up at our small town's meetings, walked me through his assessment of Our Floor Situation.

"I didn't know we had a Floor Situation," I said as I shoveled cereal into my mouth.

"Option A," he replied sternly after sipping his coffee and placing the light gray mug with black, ironic "This meeting sucks" lettering on it, on the table. "Pay a ridiculous amount of money to install carpet wall to wall."

"Uh-huh," I replied.

"Option B," he offered with a furrowed brow. "Get a still very expensive custom-sized rug to fill the entire floor since it's not a standard size."

"OK," I said, wondering if the difference between a custom rug and a custom carpet is like the difference between a padded bra and breast implants, where one just lays on top while the other gets permanently affixed.

"And option C," Jesse asserted. "Order a cheapo, wrongly sized, crappy toxic rug [my words, not his], sight unseen."

I paused—the amount of time I guesstimated gave the impression that I was considering Our Floor Situation with as much thoughtfulness as I'd given to my Grow Out My Terrible Layers Cut by a Dangerously Persuasive New Hair Stylist Who Said They'd Make My Hair Easier to Style but Was Full of Shit Conundrum. Then I told Jesse that I agreed option A seemed like an unnecessary use of funds, but I couldn't offer input on options B and C without actually touching rugs to understand the differences better.

He looked at me as if I had said we were out of dish soap while he was eating off a fork I'd let my dog lick clean instead.

I reminded him that I can't make decisions without involving all of my senses. He should've remembered when I couldn't pick a bathtub without getting into it in the store (he was in the right to stop me from getting nude in Home Depot for the full bathing effect) and how I couldn't choose a wedding cake without three tastings or a mattress without a scabies scare.

He looked at me and said, "Why do you need to go roll around on a bunch of carpet samples to make a decision?"

Five free-shipping days later, I'm rolling around on a gray, lightly toxic carpet with off-white embossed stars and a ninety-day return policy.

On the other side of the nursery, Jesse, too, is face down on the carpet. His left eye, cheek, and measuring tape are sideways in a critical investigation of which increment of one eighth of an inch would be the primo thickness for a rug pad over which the closet door can still open.

I turn over to lie on my back, where my daughter's crib will soon be stationed, and my eyes meet the ceiling. There's a crack and some faded markings where the former owner's light fixtures have been patched up.

Suddenly I time-traveled to my childhood room with my younger self back on my bed. All these years later, the image of my off-white ceiling covered in stucco popcorn stayed intact in my mind's eye like an old friend. And with that ceiling above came a familiar feeling within: a pit in my stomach, a lump in my throat, and a question in my head—am I broken?

I embarked on a mental road trip, bringing myself back below all sorts of ceilings from my past. I saw my first college dorm room, where the ceiling reflected my loneliness; then my first college apartment, with a new view but the same feeling; and then my second college apartment, too.

I flashed back to a couple of college boys' beds, where I'd

stare up, dehydrated and dizzy and full of Bud Light, wondering if this was the "college dream" I'd been told to expect.

I saw ceilings of summer where, amid the endless black, above me was the moon and some shooting stars and the overwhelming feeling of insignificance.

I recalled the ceiling above early career-girl Talia, which reflected the ambition in my eyes right back at me, and then the later successful Talia, suddenly comfortable with the two essential forms of currencies (dollars and followers), who gazed up wondering if this is what success was supposed to feel like. *Maybe success is like cilantro,* I thought. *Maybe to some people it just tastes like soap.*

When I think about the ceilings I've looked at, I recall the thoughts that kept me awake. Sometimes I'd be brainstorming how I could try again to fix myself. Other times I'd be overcome by shame for how broken I was. I'd lay in feelings of fear that I was beyond repair or send secular cries up there for help.

I can't remember the first time I felt broken. I think it was during moments I'd question why something that was supposed to make me happy did not make me happy. Eventually this incongruency built up enough that it became unignorable, strengthening in all sorts of surprising ways.

Like every time I'd pass a magazine headline at the grocery store checkout counter telling me "Three Ways to Be Happier NOW!" I didn't need to be a word nerd to understand that the -*er* on the end of *happy* insinuated that I wasn't currently happy enough. I also didn't need the added anxiety that if I didn't get that magazine, I would miss out on the three ways to be happier and would be less happy forever. And this was just a trip to the grocery store.

Sometimes I'd brainstorm what more I needed to do to get it right, to feel satisfied. Work harder? Have more gratitude?

Even though none of them were mirrors (except for that one Sigma Chi fraternity guy's), those ceilings seemed to reflect my deepest truth right back at me every night: I don't matter. And then, if I don't matter, what does?

I've spent much of my life hoping to find an answer to my inscrutable angst by connecting the glow-in-the-dark stars on the ceiling, and I'm far from alone.

One day, my daughter is going to lie on her back staring up at this ceiling, inevitably feeling broken in some way. How many hours will she spend with this view, her eyes concentrated on the white plaster, wrestling with herself? Will she, too, wish to "just be normal"? Oh god. Would sorrow over her own insignificance take space in her sweet head like it did mine?

And I got to thinking: How do we wind up looking at ceilings for clues on how to fix ourselves? What gets us to that place?

I pictured my beautiful daughter lying here someday looking up at the same cracks and rings in this ceiling. I imagined a perfect little human lying on her back, snuggly swaddled like a burrito, with her perfect teeny eyes squeezed closed. I envisioned her growing inside a world that, no matter what, will tell her she needs to fix herself. Tears welled in my own eyes as I imagined that one day she would gaze at this ceiling afraid that she'll never fix herself enough. Wondering how she could change so that she could feel happy. Learning to doubt me when I'd say, "You're enough just the way you are."

I wanted to shield my daughter from allowing the world to wind her up like a windup toy and instruct her to march toward . . . something—ANYTHING. And I wanted to block my baby's minuscule ears from being told the ways she's broken.

Looking back, I realized it was almost like once I fit into

kid shoes, the kind with soles that actually had treads, I was shoved into a wedding conga line and required to keep up with everyone else moving forward, forced smiles on all of our faces.

Cynthia, the hypnobirthing instructor, had explained all sorts of things about bringing a baby into the world. One thing she hadn't touched on, however, was how our perfect baby would inevitably grow to learn her ABCs and 123s and to feel broken. Is dissatisfaction in our tap water?

At that moment, I resolved to understand how I could help exempt my daughter from a life of lying awake, counting her flaws like sheep. Driven by that concern, I committed to not letting her throw away a minute trying to be someone she's not—or feeling shame about the someone she is. I don't think I could handle the image of my daughter lulling herself to sleep with the soundtrack of self-criticism, or worse, self-hatred. Because far too much of my own life has been wasted staring achingly at the ceiling berating myself and believing I was broken, and I needed to figure out how to make her apple fall many, many football fields away from my tree.

So, in the time it took to go from imagining her crib to seeing her stand in it (three years), I got down and dirty in both mental health research and diapers. I became physically and mentally exhausted from both a lack of sleep and an excess of philosophy. I shed tears of joy for the innate perfection of my child (and all children) and tears of fear for her (and their) future in a culture that is getting increasingly better at convincing them the opposite.

I believe I've patched together a coherent ethos that can set her, me, you, and future generations free. This book is a little longer than *Goodnight Moon*, but I hope it can have a similar effect: a peaceful night's sleep dreaming of bears in chairs and kittens with mittens instead of ways to improve yourself in order to be happier and more normal.

NORMAL

I used to sit around and wonder what life would be like if I were normal. When you're normal, do single socks never vanish in the wash? Does dairy never give you diarrhea? How do you scan a bar for all the abnormals, lest you buy one of them a drink?!

Our culture's threshold for being abnormal is criminally low. You're not normal if becoming a parent isn't in your future. Getting a shiny engagement ring didn't bring you fulfillment? Abnormal! And you're off your goddamn rocker if you're content with your career. Don't you want more? You have so much potential!

Normal is the benchmark around which we orient ourselves. It's like how 32 degrees is the point that separates freezing from not: there's Normal° and there's not, and we've learned to stick a thermometer in everything about ourselves and calculate our degrees away from that point.

Now, let's not confuse Normal° with conventional. Particularly post-coronavirus pandemic, what used to be seen as "unconventional lifestyles" are today much more widely accepted. More and more people are working hybrid, a huge change from only a few years ago when the conventional lifestyle was to go to a workplace every day. More couples are opting for no weddings, minimal weddings, elopement weddings, or Zoom weddings (because nothing says "I love you" like "Can you hear me now?"). And a space for one's pronouns has been added to everything from working professionals' business email signatures to hospital medical forms.

Unconventional is different from abnormal. *Abnormality* can be defined as a deviation from "ideal" mental health, while *unconventional* pertains to deviations from common cultural lifestyle choices.

The distinction lies in intentionally versus inadvertently deviating from societal norms.

Today, if a ten-year-old boy wants to wear a unicorn helmet and tutu, he's unconventional and mainly accepted. But if he doesn't smile when he's given that unicorn helmet as a gift from his aunt Mary, well, he's worryingly not normal.

The awful paradox is that we often don't know we're abnormal until we're told we're abnormal, mainly by the constant influx of help we're offered (or sold) to fix us. And frighteningly, the message is covert. You can be kicking back with a kombucha and a *20/20* rerun and suddenly get a pop-up on your phone that says, "Seven Signs You Don't Exercise Hard Enough," and now you realize that, damn, you're totally exercising less hard than Normal°.

"Upgrade Your Mindset: How to Think like a Success" → I must not be thinking like a success.

"Master Your Time: Productivity Hacks for a More Fulfilling Life" → My life isn't fulfilling enough. I'm not good at time management. I need to be more productive.

"Reinvent Yourself: Strategies for a Fresh Start" → You're right, I need to scratch this whole "me" thing and start over at this self thing.

"Unlock Your Inner Confidence: Tips for Boosting Self-Esteem" → Am I not confident enough? Are others more confident than me?

"Maximize Your Happiness: Simple Ways to Find Joy Every Day" → I do not find a normal amount of joy each day.

Whatever way it's framed—*don't, mistake, wrong, abnormal, better*—the avenues of help are the same. Fix. Improve. Change. GET CLOSER TO NORMAL°.

In his beautiful memoir, *The Reason I Jump*, Naoki Higashida shares: "When I was small, I didn't even know that I was a kid with special needs. How did I find out? By other people telling me that I was different from everyone else, and that this was a problem."[1] The subtitle of Higashida's book is *The Inner Voice of a Thirteen-Year-Old Boy with Autism*, so the difference he's depicting takes place on what is presently named the neurodiversity spectrum, which is an organizational tool for the various degrees of neurological abnormality. "True enough," Higashida acknowledges. "It was very hard for me to act like a normal person."

But whether we're talking about being neurotypical or emotionally typical, the only way to be atypical is to *accept* that there is a "typical."

And typical or Normal° is something as unique to a community as, say, a preferred coffee chain. "Boundary lines are drawn more by culture than nature," cultural anthropologist Roy Richard Grinker writes. In Italy, moody children can be considered "expressive," whereas in Sweden the same youngsters may be called "difficult" for requiring so much attention. In Japan, direct eye contact can be considered disrespectful, whereas in America it's considered the most respectful. While American babies are evaluated early on eye contact—and are rushed to a specialist if they don't hit those milestones—Japanese kids are taught to avoid it. Every society invents its own spectrums, from what is considered normal behavior to what are considered normal beverages. It's also been proved ad nauseam that our cultures color our opinions. And not even necessarily the culture whose soil we were born on! Psychologists have found that even if we move, we change to our new culture's opinions more easily than we can change to our new culture's accent.

I grew up in the 1990s, when the main societal pressures centered on magazine ads were to *get milk!* and maybe invest in some "Chicken Soup for the Soul," and I was still up at night with agonizing fear and self-criticism about whether I was doing life right. Today, via our armor of digital devices and social media, we're pinged with auto-reminders of what we don't have, and constantly see people showing off what they do have. Given our competitors (all other humans) and our incompetence (all things), it's truly a miracle any of us get out of bed at all. (And we probably have the wrong sheets anyway: Silk? Organic? Linen? Not been fresh for two weeks?) We can't stroll through a grocery store or scroll down a social media feed without getting a nudge (or a command) to pull ourselves closer to Normal°. Work harder! Dream bigger! Eat better! Red light! Green light!

And for what? What is this all for?

That must be a rhetorical question, right? For happiness. Of course. Happiness is *the* 32 degrees Fahrenheit set point (or zero degrees Celsius). That's the point at which happiness is normal, and all roads must lead to happiness.

We're swimming in a cultural sea of "happiness = normalcy."

Author David Foster Wallace shared this little ditty with the Kenyon College graduating class in a now-famed 2005 commencement speech: "There are these two young fish swimming along and they happen to meet an older fish swimming the other way, who nods at them and says, 'Morning, boys. How's the water?'

"And the two young fish swim on for a bit, and then eventually one of them looks over at the other and goes, 'What the hell is water?'"

Water, I'd tell the fishes if we had a meet-cute on some coral reef, is our deep-rooted belief that happiness is the norm. Our value meter is set to units of happiness. Western culture idolizes happiness. We've made it the number one goal of life. We've turned the human experience into a mission of avoiding pain and maximizing pleasure. The polluted pursuit of happiness is so ingrained in us that we don't even realize we're dog-paddling in it. And if we do happen to pull back from our school (of fish) to stop to notice the water—if we pause in the quiet stillness of the night to hear our soul whisper, *Is this all there is to life?*— well then, we're unequivocally an abnormal flounder who needs an immediate professional repairperson. There are two main types:

1. Licensed mental health professionals/therapists
2. Self-help experts

In American football there are two squads per team: the offensive lineup and the defensive lineup, both of whose goals are to win by beating the other team (if you needed a little refresher on sports for this upcoming analogy).

In the game of life, with happiness being the ultimate "win," there's a squad playing the role of the defensive lineup. These players are skilled defenders who tackle emotional and mental distress head-on, aiming to prevent it from taking over and disrupting the game. They analyze, treat, and sometimes even diagnose issues, much like defensive players intercepting passes or stopping the opponent's advance.

Meanwhile, there's also an offensive line of players who charge forward, armed with positivity and affirmations. With enviable gusto, offensive players bulldoze through life's challenges, shouting, "No pain, no gain!" and "Happiness is a choice!" and "My thoughts create my reality!" as they barrel toward the end zone of eternal bliss, dodging self-doubt like a nimble quarterback evading a sack.

Each squad's distinct strategies mainly arise from the fact that they have been coached differently.

Let's discuss how these two types of happiness repairpeople have been taught to do damage control.

Defensive Lineup

There's a required class for all psychology majors called Abnormal Psychology, where they dissect the peculiarities of human emotion with all the subtlety of a sledgehammer to a watermelon. In Abnormal Psych, one thing they study is depression (pronounced "dee-presh-un" for those of you new to this "abnormal" condition), that exotic condition characterized by persistent feelings of sadness and hopelessness and loss of interest in activities you once enjoyed. Thankfully, the condition is so abnormal that it manages to ensnare, at minimum, only a measly 20 percent of the population every year.

Another hot topic in Abnormal Psychology is this unfortunate condition called anxiety. Have you heard of it? It's a condition so rare that it affects a mere 40 million adults, which is equivalent only to the total population of New York, Ohio, and New Jersey combined. An abnormality, this anxiety thing.

In Abnormal Psych, abnormality isn't about being, well, abnormal in the unconventional sense like we discussed before—like wearing a bra outside your clothes to brunch, raising your family of four in a converted school bus, or pushing your puppy in a baby stroller. What we may consider "uncommon behavior" is not necessarily abnormality. Abnormal in this textbook sense is anything that causes issues in someone's life. The baseline for a "normal" human experience is floating through life like a carefree butterfly, completely devoid of distress. Normal = no pathology. (Apparently.)

In other words, the more distress caused by one's own patterns of emotion, thought, and behavior, the more abnormality. The less anguish, the more usual.

So, by those measures, do you know one single normal person? Scientists don't, either. In one study that spanned three decades, 83 percent of participants fit the bill for having one to three "abnormal" disorders. The report noted, "This pattern suggests that the 'typical' human experience is one characterized by at least one brush with a diagnosable disorder, and that those who avoid these conditions entirely . . . are actually quite rare."[2] Right. It turns out that being entirely disorder-free is about as common as finding a spa-like porta-potty.

With one out of every five people on an antidepressant, and 40 percent of American adults affected by an anxiety disorder, *abnormal* isn't the first adjective I'd employ to describe such states of mind. Classifying these conditions as abnormal is like teaching gluten sensitivity in a class called Bizarre Dietetics.

Plus, the psychological solutions to our abnormalities

aren't necessarily eliminating them. While these psychological solutions keep improving and expanding as medication and therapy become more widespread, our mental health crisis is also becoming more widespread. When, to be clear, we should be seeing the opposite result.

Offensive Lineup

While mental health professionals receive their training from accredited institutions, self-help or personal development experts attend the school of life.

The message of these life DIY-ers is more or less the same: you can control your thoughts. Instead of using clinical terms like "mental illness" or "abnormalities," self-help lingo calls these conditions "limiting beliefs," "self-sabotage," or "fear." The focus is on empowering us to overcome and blast past barriers to achieve our full potential and unlock our best selves.

These are the experts who tell us that we're in the driver's seat. So if (and when) we don't feel magnificent, it's we who have failed—and it's we who need to work harder and harder and shout our affirmations louder and louder and meditate until we have butt blisters and maybe change our wall colors or our coffee sweetener or our husband's beard until we finally once and for all FIX OURSELVES INTO HAPPY.

So, most of us awaken to alarms, wash the sleepies out of our eyes, brush our teeth, and set off to will our worries away. We turn to positivity apps, advice articles, and bright-eyed influencers who reassure us in cheerful colors, whimsical fonts, and peppy phrasing enveloped in exclamation points that happiness is simply a choice and/or an easy result of yanking toxic people (and shampoo) (and limiting beliefs) from our orbit!

Within the self-help sphere, nothing poses a greater roadblock to our best life than a negative mindset.

But if self-help actually helped, the most likely customer for a new self-help book wouldn't be someone who'd bought a similar self-help book within the preceding eighteen months. It's one thing to buy gardening book after gardening book because you have a passion for forsythias, but it's another thing to buy *How to Be So Happy* a few months after *How to Be Less Miserable*.

So, if we go back to when we were fish a few pages ago, what if we happened to sit in the quiet stillness of a coral reef and question whether happiness is truly the whole point, and we weren't considered an abnormal flounder who needs an immediate professional repairperson? What if, in those moments of coral-based contemplation, an eel slithered up to us and whispered in our ears, "Nothing's wrong with you, my friend. You're just having the normal living-creature experience."

Of course it's natural to ruminate with worry, anxiety, and fear—these are your run-of-the-mill side effects of humaning. But that inescapable feeling of being defective, broken, pointless, in need of fixing—well, that is human-made.

To be alive is to be anxious. To be anxious is to be alive. This is the emotional version of *Everybody Poops*.

So, what if society's definition of *normal* is what's really abnormal? What then?

Because I'll tell you what's the most abnormal—someone who's never experienced anxiety, depression, phobias, compulsiveness, OCD, addiction, and so on. Someone who's never had emotional anguish. The fact that we're pitched fixes to our "abnormal" problems is not only backward but is also what teaches us that these normal human conditions are easy to fix—or fixable at all. As cultural anthropologist Roy Richard Grinker writes in his landmark book *Nobody's Normal*, "Nobody's normal."

Grinker's grandfather was a psychiatrist who was also a patient of Dr. Freud's in Vienna. Grandfather Grinker told grandson Grinker that Freud's wish was that doctors could focus on helping patients not live a perfect life, but live one of "ordinary unhappiness." Freud wanted to prove that emotional distress was universal, and that maybe some psychiatric conditions could become as mainstream and benign as the common cold or seasonal allergies: something we all get from time to time that doesn't cause us to go running into hiding and dissolving in shame and dishing out our savings on self-help seminars.

Everyone has at least a smidge of mental illness. Emotional pain is a normal part of life. Speaking about his magnum opus, *The Myth of Normal*, Dr. Gabor Maté powerfully argues that being considered "normal" requires accepting some deeply unhealthy standards. "Illness itself, whether of mind or body, is in many cases a normal response to abnormal circumstances," he said. "So *The Myth of Normal* means . . . that what we consider to be the norm is neither healthy or natural . . . [and] what we consider abnormal in terms of illness is often a normal response to unhealthy circumstances."[3]

So I propose a flip-flop. If nobody's normal, and everyone's at minimum a little abnormal, I propose we rebrand abnormal as normal.

We're looking at this entire kit and caboodle off-kilter. I believe that feeling less broken and in need of fixing comes from embracing the universal human condition as Normal°.

I think it's likely that we're trying to treat the symptoms of a soulful problem with medical remedies, and that if we peered through the lens of philosophy, we might be able to make major headway in feeling better.

Philosophy offers a more soothing approach to human suffering.

Philosophy doesn't see emotional discomfort as a flaw to be corrected, but rather as a norm to be accepted.

And no philosophers had their finger on the pulse of our inner turmoil quite like the existentialists. This group has a lineage that dates back to the nineteenth century, though some date existential thought back to Aristotle. Those we put at the forefront of existential philosophy passed the baton like they were running a relay, one picking up where another left off, expanding and modifying the prior's thoughts with the times.

Existentialism is that special friend you turn to for actual guidance and love. Not the friend who tells you, without bothering to look, that the final-sale bridesmaid's dress looks perfect. Not the friend who texts you when you're scared that your dog might have cancer to promise "Duke will be all right, sweetie." Not even the friend who, when your relationship goes south, buys you shots and scours the bar for a revenge beau.

No. Existentialism is the pal that says, "Honestly, I think the A-line dress is more your ass's speed." And when you say the one you have is non-exchangeable, replies, "Ah well, fuck." Empathy. Existentialism is the friend that cries with you when Duke is potentially sick, and that teases she told you so when a new relationship goes south. Existentialism is frank, genuine, fair, compassionate, practical, and brutally honest. Existentialism is realistic, strong, resilient, and deep.

When understood and, most important, acted upon correctly, you'll never meet a more empowering and practical ideology than existentialism.

Existentialists knew that what we are really doing when we

lie in bed at night, snuggled on our Casper mattresses in our Brooklinen sheets staring up at our lead-free painted ceilings, is trying to steady ourselves. As the father of existentialism, philosopher Søren Kierkegaard, famously said, "Anxiety is the dizziness of freedom."

HOW TO NOT SELF-HELP

It was tricky writing a how-to-quit-self-help book without writing a self-help book.

Instead, I tried to write a how-to-think-existentially book, which I believe checks both of the boxes above. Existentialism helps us quit self-help by reminding us that there are no simple, one-size-fits-all solutions to life's inevitable challenges. "The crowd is untruth," Kierkegaard said, which is why our struggles won't be fixed at a motivational conference, in a bestselling book, or by a viral TikTok therapist.

What I appreciate about the existential philosophers is their framework for tackling life's toughest questions. Even though they tell us bluntly that we must make our own decisions (Jean-Paul Sartre says man is fully responsible for his own existence), it's comforting to be given a vocabulary for processing these difficult topics. Existentialism lets us see life from a different perspective.

In a lot of ways, looking at life existentially is like looking at life through a fish-eye lens: it challenges our conventional understanding of reality. Our perspective gets warped in unique and unexpected ways. Through this lens, the familiar becomes unfamiliar, the ordinary becomes extraordinary, and we're pushed to question what's real, exaggerated, and confusing. The lens reminds us that life is not merely a passive observation but an active engagement with our own existence.

The existential lens bends reality, highlighting the profound and often overlooked aspects of our lives. It magnifies the complexities and uncertainties that lie beneath the surface, urging us to confront the fundamental questions of our existence. It reveals the absurdities, paradoxes, and existential angst that can accompany our journey.

What if those of us labeled "abnormal" are actually born with innate existential lenses? What if our resistance to conformity isn't a flaw but a sign that we've seen through the social BS, making it impossible to fit into the cookie-cutter molds?

When author Steven Pressfield explained his time spent in a halfway house to podcast host Tim Ferris, Pressfield said: "You would think that people were really struggling mentally, but in fact, the people in this halfway house . . . were among the smartest people that I ever met and the funniest and the most interesting. And what I concluded from hanging out with them and from others in a similar situation was that they weren't crazy at all, that they were actually the smart people who had sort of seen through the bullshit, and because of that, they couldn't function in the world. They couldn't hold a job because they just couldn't take the bullshit, and that was how they wound up in institutions, because the greater society thought, 'Well these people are absolute rejects. They can't fit in.' But in fact to my mind, they were actually the people that really saw through everything."

So, what if we Abnormal° people are people with existential fish lenses? What if that's why we can't force ourselves to be Normal° or fixed—despite following the guides?

That's what I want to teach my daughter because that's what set me free.

Acceptance.

Acceptance of the unchangeable angst that comes as a

two-for-one deal with our existence. Which is what stopped me from lying in bed searching in the stucco for a cure for the human condition.

EXISTENTIALISH

Existentialish is my chill take on a complex philosophical movement about the nature and meaning of human existence. Existentialish is relishing in the relief that so much in life is loosey-goosey. For existentialists, we're doing life properly if we're uncomfortable as hell.

I know, finally! A group of people who tell us it's Normal° to feel so untethered that we need a couple of pints of ice cream to ease the emotional turmoil that comes from the dizziness of freedom, the burden of responsibility, the pressure that we ultimately become nothing more than what we decide to be through our actions. (They would also tell us if ice cream gives us meaning, grab a spoon.)

When I accepted this worldview, I felt unfathomable relief. Life is meant to be uncomfortable and I am meant to feel anxious. Dizziness and nausea, angst and dread, are the natural symptoms of embracing and choosing freedom, and they may not always be remedied by weekly co-pays with a kind, licensed counselor, by swallowing pills from the CVS pharmacy drive-through, or by reading a ghostwritten book by a well-branded guru. Though they can be! There's no shame if therapy or self-help does help. And this is not a rallying cry to toss your Lexapro out the window. This is a simply a persuasion to look deeper and to say that if there's something that isn't resonating for you in the way you're being diagnosed and treated, know you're so far from alone. Others like you could fill a Taylor Swift concert venue three hundred times over.

I believe that what we call a mental health crisis can also be called an existential crisis—that we're pinning a clinical phrase on a philosophical struggle.

Existentialism encourages us to, as Marino puts it, "reach through the suffering, the anxiety, the inexplicable sadness instead of always looking for the express lane out of that numbing and ever-deepening feeling that nothing matters." Existentialism is realism. It's acknowledge-ism. It's accept-ism. As Kierkegaard famously wrote, "We can be deceived by believing what is untrue, but we certainly are also deceived by not believing what is true."

We're egged on from every angle to be freethinkers and to follow our passions and dreams and callings and purposes while also receiving instructions to do so in a certain way. We're told via blogs, podcasts, and social media posts to live carefree in a van and climb mountains! Be yourself! But also, you have to be yourself on Instagram and make other people want to be you, too. And then if enough people wish that instead of working at a daycare they, too, could be climbing mountains and living in a van, you'll get free van mattresses. Not to mention free gear and other shit. And then eventually, you'll in turn get these products out in the universe so that you may even be able to replace your van with a new Mercedes. I bet someone would totally be down to be your driver so they can see how you've monetized your passion. It's the perfect life!

The contradictions that we absorb every day can cause us So. Much. Misery.

On the surface, my daughter may like that she never needs to wonder what the people she met on vacation in Miami are eating after their intermittent fast—it's on social media. Though she'll be constantly worrying if she should be intermittent fasting, too.

I have a hunch that people got fed up with what Sartre called "the burden of responsibility." I think people said, "Fuck this. I don't want to have to DECIDE what to eat or wear or be when I grow up. It's so much easier just following what Kim Kardashian does."

But instead of feeling stressed about the overwhelming choice of what to make of our lives, we follow blindly and in turn no longer develop a personal value system.

We claim personal brand names, but we don't stop to actually think about, talk about, or try on what makes life feel MEANINGFUL to us. Is it creativity? Freedom? Family? Career? Independence? These are questions we may forget to pause to answer. Because whether it's God's doing or nature or nurture, we are naturally wired a certain way.

But the odd part is that it's not always easy to be aware of or understand our wiring. It'd be a whole lot easier if information throughout our life was recorded like a birth (time of birth, birth weight and length, and decibel of screaming). If at some point in our lives someone jotted down other specific characteristics, like we get energy from being alone (introvert) or we're susceptible to giant mood swings (bipolar) or dairy makes us break out. All the things.

We are required to scavenger-hunt our identity. Maybe that's the whole point?

But we are not taught or told or encouraged to do this. We are told simply, "THESE ARE THE JEANS WE WEAR IN OUR TOWN."

It takes courage (and curiosity) to allow ourselves to question who we are. More courage than it does to just do what we swipe and see. Not into working the family business? Feeling pulled to take off to live in France? Just decided that the home you've been saving for isn't for you? It takes guts to do that deep self-examination . . . and then taking action might feel uncomfortable, too.

Our values dictate our choices every day—big and small. And our choices create our life—one and only. So this is kind of a life-or-death situation.

And the tragic, terrible, terrifying part is that it's increasingly becoming a death situation. I believe that the times we are living in can be considered a "meaningless epidemic." Deaths dubbed "deaths of despair" are increasing at an alarming rate; these are deaths related to drugs, alcohol, and suicide (the former two, in my opinion, are just slower versions of the latter). They often stem from feelings of hopelessness, emptiness, and gloom, and thoughts of a life void of any meaning.

I believe that if we spent time on inner work and moving toward meaning instead of just copying and pasting ideas from social media, we'd be in better shape.

So rather than slather new advice on top of ye olde self-help advice you're already covered in, my approach is to give you new glasses. Not rose-colored ones like our culture gives us at birth, but ones with a different lens—that existentialish fish-eye lens I mentioned earlier. Because relooking at life through an existentialish lens has changed everything for me, and I will argue, regardless of your religious affiliation (or lack of), it's the healthiest way to look at our existence.

In addition to a new lens, I'm going to help you understand the forces that keep us swirling in a cyclone of societal pressure. Because only if we understand our history can we fight the wind that creates our present and exist in a new way.

This is a book about how adopting an existentialish philosophy can help you accept both yourself and the complexities of the human condition. I hope to provide you with a trapdoor out of the maze of self-help trends that may offer you fleeting solace but ultimately fail to soothe the depths of your inner turmoil.

Existentialish thought helped me realize that what I believed were my own flaws or faults were, in reality, a piercing clarity slicing through the facade of societal expectation. It is this philosophy that encourages us to look life's absurdities square in the eyes like we've been approached by a bear, rather than run and hide from them like someone avoiding their own shadow. Through an existentialish lens, you can embrace life's loosey-goosey nature and expect the dizziness that comes from being a free person.

In this book I share what I've learned, not as a guide to becoming normal or fixed, but as a celebration of our inherent abnormality. It's a journey of acceptance, embracing the unchangeable angst that comes bundled with our existence, a package deal we can't opt out of.

As Simone de Beauvoir wisely remarked, "The world may be chaotic and unpredictable, but it is through embracing the inherent uncertainty that we can find authenticity, freedom, and the opportunity to shape our own lives." This, my friends, is the lesson that set me free, and it's what I aspire to teach my daughter—a lesson in acceptance, not only of the world around us but of ourselves, freeing us from the endless search for a cure to the human condition. Get ready for an exploration that goes beyond the surface, for a journey that starts with acceptance and leads to the profound wisdom hidden within the echoes of an awakening.

Existentialist thought argues that we're meant to feel scared and seasick because life is risky and nauseating. That because we have endless options for how to live, but only one life to live, it's a wee bit of a high-pressure situation to make choices—especially given that whatever we do will shape our present and future and trickle into others' presents and futures in completely unpredictable and uncontrollable ways. Sartre called this crushing pressure to create our life with our every decision "the burden of responsibility." Not "the gift of adulting duties!" or the "delight of relentless personal accountability!" or "an opportunity for manifestation." No. Sartre said we're "condemned to be free." Not blessed, not fortunate, not charmed.

So, imagine if we paradigm-shifted. Imagine if inner emotional disturbances like depression, anxiety, and grief weren't taught in Abnormal Psychology class but instead were accepted—embraced, even, as the normal reality of human nature. Imagine if statistics about the increasingly concerning growth of our collective mental health hitting the shitter didn't bombard us on the daily like it's breaking news. We can be heartbroken, of course, at the increasingly younger onset of severe mental health symptoms. We should be fearful for our fellow humans' individual and collective well-being when we read another headline about our skyrocketing suicide rates. But to act surprised, like this is new information, is like pretending to be surprised when you arrive at a surprise party you already found out about.

So, what is the problem with being a person? The problem is that life has no inherent meaning, and if you stare that in the face, you can go batshit crazy.

As Buffy the Vampire Slayer said, "The hardest thing in this world is to live in it."

2

. . . .

Divine ~~Intervention~~ Indoctrination

I was led to my first self-help book by divine intervention (or razor-sharp marketing). The author had been an alumna of my university and had sent a copy of their book to the student newspaper (of which I was an editor) for promotion. I saw the cover and had an instant visceral hard pass.

Something about the embossed bright lettering and their goddess-like stance on the cover did not summon my soul. So I literally tossed the book to another writer, assigned them the story, and went on with my life.

I got dumped a few weeks later, just days before college graduation, and not long before he and I were set to move from New York to California to start our lives together. The perfect storm of heartbreak and impending adulthood crashed down on me like a tidal wave of fear and desperation. I remember sobbing, sprawled out on the floor, when suddenly, like a celestial messenger descending from the heavens, that book popped into my head, with the author's goddess-like stance appearing in my mind's eye like a Jehovah's Witness at a front door.

All of a sudden my visceral hard pass felt like a huge mistake. (It wasn't.)

Now, in the midst of my sorrow, this book coming into my life felt undeniably like serendipity (or apophenia: the game of connect-the-dots our desperate brains can play to assign meaningfulness to the randomness of life when we're scared shitless and yearning for certainty and stability).

So I picked myself up off the floor and tearfully made my way to the student bookstore to heed the call.

Future me would learn that "heeding the call" is a common entry into cultish ideologies. Eleven years later, I'd hear cult-deprogramming expert and author Steven Hassan explain how it's not unusual for someone to become involved with a cult when they come across something random that matches their life situation. Apparently, it's easy for us to misattribute causality like this.

For Hassan, his heeding led him to attend what he would afterward understand to be an indoctrination retreat for the Moonies cult. He tells the story of how he was sitting in his college cafeteria mourning a recent breakup (sounds familiar) when some pretty girls (also familiar) came up to him to invite him to a fun event. Hassan said, "They started with 'We're going away this weekend. We're gonna have a great time.' . . . And I'm like, 'I'm a banquet waiter. I work on the weekends. I have never had a weekend off for two years. Please stop asking me to come.' . . . And they kept bugging me."

So Hassan succumbed to their pressure, telling them that if for some reason (which he didn't expect in a million years) he happened to not work that weekend, he'd join them.

And whaddayaknow, two days later, Hassan said, "I call

up my boss. . . . He said, 'You won't believe it, but the wedding was called off. Take the weekend off.'" And boom. Call heeded. In self-help speak, this is called synchronicity: the universe's way of communicating with us. Synchronicity is sternly differentiated from chance. In fact, self-help authors argue that there are no mistakes, no coincidences, and that everything that happens is a signal from the divine, guiding us toward our highest destiny.

Synchronicity rests its hat on there being a deeper underlying order or interconnectedness in the universe, where events align in a meaningful way beyond mere chance or causality. The term *synchronicity* was given significance by Swiss psychologist Carl Jung in the 1920s. It's said that Jung was talking with a patient who was recounting a dream about a golden scarab beetle when he heard a tapping sound at the window. When he opened the window, the same beetle described in the dream flew in! Jung was in awe of the coincidence and pondered the idea of flukes that couldn't be explained logically—he believed these remarkable "in sync" moments showed the hidden ties between us and the cosmos and suggested we view them as signs of a deeper order or intelligence in the universe.

In fancy psychobabble, this is called apophenia: the human instinct to assign meaning to coincidences in your life, to see patterns or connections in disorder or randomness.

Apophenia is when you look at a cloud and see the logo of the company that offered you a job that you were unsure of taking, but your friend just sees a fluffy white blob. Or when you stare at the knots in a piece of wood and think they spell out the name of your ex, whom you clearly must call right now. It's when your brain makes connections between random, unrelated things, like an enthusiastic, but slightly deluded detective searching for patterns in everything from traffic lights to latte foam in order to help you make sense of this wild rodeo of a world.

Seeing the world as a wild rodeo is what existentialists call "absurdity." Absurdity describes how goofy they feel it is to try to impose order and clarity on what they describe as an "irrational" world—a world without logic, pattern, or structure. A world that, no offense, operates without any inherent meaning, purpose, or concern for human life. Yes, it follows physical laws (gravity!) but has no consciousness or intention behind it. Basically, entrepreneurial existentialists would likely sell key chains reading "Everything does not happen for a reason" or "Cosmic plan, shmosmic plan."

ABSURDITY

You know that perplexing feeling of sitting alone in your room thinking of something you crave? *Bagel. Bagel. Bagel. Bagel.* And then, at some point, the word *bagel* loses any familiar meaning and becomes a source of complete bewilderment?

And then, because you're obviously now craving one, you grab a package of bagels, and the once-familiar word appears foreign, and its letters b-a-g-e-l take on the appearance of cryptic symbols?!

Well, this is what existential philosophers refer to as the absurd. Except rather than the word *bagel* transforming itself into an incomprehensible entity, for them, it's l-i-f-e that evokes a sense of disorientation and prompts us to question the very fabric of existence.

This is absurdity. It's the contemplation and then the realization that when we *really* think about it, there are a *lot* of fundamental uncertainties and paradoxes that underpin what we've thought was our reality.

In existentialism, absurdity is when we zoom out and describe the world as being illogical and strange, unreliable and hard.

Long before existentialists called it an absurdity, the notion of the unpredictable and arbitrary nature of life was described in the Bible. Ecclesiastes 9:11 highlights that despite our efforts or attributes, there is no guarantee of success, as chance and unexpected events can overtake everyone. This recognition of life's uncertainties and the lack of direct correlation between effort and outcome resonates with the existentialist notion of the absurd.

> I have seen something further under the sun, that the swift do not always win the race, nor do the mighty win the battle, nor do the wise always have the food, nor do the intelligent always have the riches, nor do those with knowledge always have success because time and unexpected events overtake them all.[1]

While a period or an exclamation point would have been a nice touch in this run-on sentence, both perspectives suggest that life is not inherently rational or structured according to our desires or expectations. They emphasize the gap between our yearning for meaning and the inherent randomness or chaos of existence. In this sense, Ecclesiastes 9:11 can be seen as aligning with existentialist ideas about the absurdity of life and the need to confront and find meaning within this absurdity.

Any way we slice it—philosophically, psychologically, biblically, or with a fancy bagel cutter—this world is unobjectively absurd. "Absurd" meaning there is no one truth; no inherent set of rules or guidelines or purposes or answers, no real reason to set our fork to the left of our plate and the knife and spoon on the right. For many, understandably, this zooming out can feel like too much.

This idea about the irrationality of the world isn't an easy one to swallow. Think about it. When you see order (or purpose or meaning) in the world, it allows you—on a very fundamental level—to feel at home, tucked under a snuggly weighted blanket of universal order. You can feel most comfortable with yourself and with your actions when they fit into some larger schema outside you. This external framework can, in a way, be comforting because it gives you assurance that a kind of glue is holding everything together and that you can just kind of let the wind blow you.

Existentialist philosopher Friedrich Nietzsche observed that our need for clarity increases in tandem with the pain of our suffering. He famously said, "To live is to suffer, to survive is to find some meaning in the suffering."[2] Like, if we miss a flight, it's way more psychologically comforting to believe that the universe helped us dodge having a really lousy seatmate than to accept the fact that now we're stuck in an airport for the next five hours.

Like looking at a solar eclipse without the cardboard glasses, viewing life as absurd can fuck you up. And I think existentialists would be empathetic to our attempt to look for dots to connect to get some iota of assistance to navigate this world! They would also nonjudgmentally understand how apophenia (or synchronicity) is our brain's way of putting a Band-Aid on this boo-boo. In *You Are Not So Smart*, David McRaney explains, "More often than not, apophenia is the result of the most dependable of all delusions—the confirmation bias. . . . When what you want to see is something meaningful, you ignore all the things in the story of your life that are meaning-less."[3]

Existentialism is consumed with the struggle between need-ing purpose and the inherent vagueness of the world. That's kind of its main thing. "The meaning of life is whatever you ascribe it to be," Sartre, or Camus, or Joseph Campbell wrote, not knowing at the time how a caveat would be needed that a targeted ad about making six figures from home by selling shampoo to your high school Facebook friends is not an en-dorsed type of ascribable meaning.

"I rebel, therefore I exist,"[4] Albert Camus once wrote, stressing the importance of being discerning in order to avoid getting taken in by false beliefs or self-help.

Because while philosophy and psychology nerds poke self-deprecating fun at how our sweet minds play self-soothing games, self-help guides capitalize on this cognitive bias. Inspi-rational guides tell us synchronicities are the universe's way of speaking to us. They tell us they can help us increase our "wow, what are the odds?!" experiences as well as decode our higher power's bread crumbs. In exchange for money. Or at least a smash of the subscribe button on their YouTube channel.

It's human nature to try to make sense of the world, and especially when we're deeply hurting we wish someone would step in to save us from the crushing weight of life. Suffering opens our hearts and doors wide open, which is why apophenia is also known as the "Jehovah's Witness effect."

So, when I reached the "alumni authors" display table at my school store, time both slowed down and sped up. The book in my hands felt like finding an umbrella in the pouring rain. My fingers tenderly caressed the embossed neon-pink title; its raised lettering raised my internal feeling of hope.

In *Cultish*, Amanda Montell maintains that it's less the feelings of desperation that lead people like me to a book like that; rather, she explains, it's an "overabundance of optimism"[5]—the promises the book (or online course or Instagram feed) sells.

Hence a voice in my head had said, "I bet she can help me," while it felt like an angel lifted me by the pom of my beanie and planted me at the checkout counter to charge $14.99 to my school account, also known as Dad.

And thus began my oxygen-level dependence on self-help literature.

Before this book entered my orbit, I had no idea that happiness had manuals. As far as my twenty-one-year-old brain and minimal life experience understood, manuals were specific step-by-step instructions for mental health and self-discovery, like comprehending a new car's navigation system, planning the most satisfying way to experience the vortexes in Sedona over a long weekend, or reupholstering a love seat you found on Craigslist in a timeless, chic, and budget-savvy way. You grab a beer and a magnifying glass and plow through the instruction manual, or you hire someone from Taskrabbit. But a manual for happiness?! An emotion?! I mean a state? Or a feeling? A value? Before I knew there were how-to manuals for it, Sephora's lipstick section would've been a more likely place to find me trying to make my mood match my lipstick name: Joy, Ethereal, Glee . . .

So finding this how-to book for a completely intangible, unmeasurable, subjective, elusive thing was the discovery of a lifetime! No one in my life had ever before promised me such an easy way to such a valuable outcome. Although teaching me how to scan in bulk with my printer came close.

It was a huge relief to realize that all I needed to do to be happy was follow a "proven method." Discovering that my discontent, distress, fear, insecurity, and unwellness were just because I'd been doing things wrong was already making me feel better. Instantly, I became substantially calmer just knowing there was a simple fix for me. A fix that could be taught in only 220 pages. It was as if I'd been straining myself trying to assemble a POÄNG armchair and then, depleted, losing hope, and hungry, I went to my menu drawer and found, buried under an oil-stained pizza-delivery menu, the step-by-step instructions for HÄPPINËSS! I was happier just by reading the back cover.

I couldn't believe I'd so incorrectly assumed that experiencing and expanding happiness was just, I don't know, something that happened to us? An evolutionary impulse like sneezing, or even an intuitive motion like high-fiving?

That assumption, I'd soon learn, was actually a major part of my problem. The book told me that happiness was something I needed to deliberately choose—like what cable provider to use. I instantly felt like a world-class idiot for not knowing that this coveted emotional state was just a choice. Do you want your latte hot, cold, or happy? Which makes my tush look better, these boyfriend jeans or happiness?

I guess I had given little thought to happiness beyond viewing it as the antithesis of all negative emotions. (Spoiler! It wasn't until later, during a therapy session when the therapist handed me a printout listing various positive feelings like pride, confidence, and admiration, that I began to realize happiness isn't the only positive emotion. I'd assumed that these other positives—like feeling comfortable, eager, or hopeful—were stepping-stones, or precursors, to happiness.)

But now I felt so silly. So naïve. So ignorant. Slightly betrayed. Here I was, about to complete year four of college. I'd majored in magazine, television, radio, and film writing. I'd minored in English. My free time was spent writing for our school newspaper. I'd read voraciously since childhood. I browsed bookstores when I felt lonely, self-soothed in libraries, and drove long distances with books on tape. How I'd spent twenty-one years of my life not knowing there were books to self-transform was beyond me. (With the exception of *The South Beach Diet* book that I believed in high school would transform me by eating handfuls of peanuts for snacks, bunless cheeseburgers for dinner, and ricotta cheese with Splenda for dessert.)

It boggles my mind that had I just forked left instead of right at my university bookstore that day, I could've found myself in a book bear hug from a bunch of fellow angsty people. People who empowered their readers to accept reality instead of cheerleading them to fix their life into a fairy tale. Had I forked left, I could have gotten a permission slip to explore life's complexities from an existentialist, instead of a simplistic formula for hacking happiness from a person I call an "expectationist."

EXPECTATIONISTS

Expectationists present happiness as a by-product of both achievement and attainment. Expectationists flaunt their happiness formulas and step-by-step guides, boasting about their Instagram-perfect lives as evidence of their expertise in fulfillment.

Expectationists create high hopes and cue us to visualize them clearly in order to get to the goal line. Goal lines are precisely where expectationists declare they will take you. Be it the goal of a fuller wallet, larger following, bigger house, smaller pant size, smarter kid, nicer garden, better grades, faster pro-motion, or sexier mate, if there is a goal line where your personal happiness is waiting, an expectationist is dying for you to pay them to lead you there in prescribed steps.

Existentialists, in contrast, are the zookeepers who, after hours, use their keys to set us animals free. They scoff at the idea of one-size-fits-all life hacks and reject the notion that happiness can be neatly packaged into a formulaic system. They'd tell you that, actually, if you want to be happier, give up reaching for total happiness, because that path inevitably leads to the opposite. (And they wouldn't shy away from telling you that taking advice from a random YouTuber or TikToker is as absurd as letting a gas station attendant write your mom's birthday card.)

From my existentialish perspective, there is no "fix" for the insurmountable challenges of being a human, because every day we're alive, we're faced with choices. And choices cause angst, especially choices that have results with stakes higher than what airline seat to pick (an excruciatingly difficult decision already!).

Existentialists look at personal responsibility in the big picture of life and meaning, while expectationists focus on ways to be better. Existentialists look at the bigger life questions, and expectationists show us how to make progress.

Existentialism is all "the burden of responsibility," which means it sucks to have to make choices for your life and to have so much free will. Self-help's energy is more like the pressure of not fucking up.

An existentialist is like, *"Hey, you're going into an ice cream place. We all know it's going to be hard. We know that at the end of the day, you're going to feel like you didn't make the right choice. Truly, whatever you choose, even if it's your best option at the moment, you know you're gonna be second-guessing and wondering what-if. And, well, it is what it is. You can only, in the words of P90X infomercial workout-video star Tony Horton, 'Do your best and forget the rest.'"*

Whereas an expectationist is like, "No, no, no, no. Listen, *if you were able to get your energy right and your thoughts in alignment, you could just walk in there and be guided to the most perfect fro-yo outcome, the most perfect concoction, and it'll feel effortless and blissful. And when you eat it, your body won't even process it as calories.*"

It's the expectations that are the huge differentiating factor. Existentialism says: *We know this sucks, it sucks for all of us, but do your best. There's no hint that some choices are superior to others. We're all out here in the weeds with you trying to do life. Bearing that in mind, carry on and be yourself.*

But in contrast, expectationists' attitude is that you can have a glorious life if you get rid of your negative thoughts: *That's all on you, girl. Keep on going until you find this utopia.* And it's a complete fantasy. It's not far off from Harry Potter. Maybe they should group self-help books with fantasy in bookstores.

Expectationists offer fixes galore. They dish out advice for those who are like, "*Gahhh! Life is so hard! Tell me exactly how I should live!!!*"

Existentialists write to those who feel "*Wahhhh? How can I possibly live in this overwhelming world?*"

Me? I am like, *Whoa, what if I'd gone to the other side of the bookstore that day?*

What if, as I was trekking tearfully toward three dozen book covers with a smiley thirty-year-old guru telling me in bright neon, embossed, whimsical letters that the answer to my unhappiness resides within her paperback, I sneezed and fell and rolled to the other side of the bookstore. What if I then stood back up in front of a small family of black-and-white books in a nondescript font, like a serif that comes standard in a Word document, staring back at me. What if one of their titles, say Man's Search for Meaning *or* The Myth of Sisyphus, *drew me in, even though I'm neither a man nor a mythology fan. And what if, instead of my only association with the term* existentialism *up until that point being depressing assigned books for which I read the SparkNotes, I had recalled having seen a neat segment on* Oprah *featuring a distant nephew of Nietzsche's shocking tell-all book revealing never-before-published juicy gossip about his great-uncle Fred?*

Of course, there's a reason this emotionally unhealthy game is called what-if. Because it's all speculation. None of that would have happened—first because sneezes don't typically roll you to the other side of bookstores, but also because existentialist philosophy books aren't the "draw you in" type.

With obscure titles, a bleak black-and-white aesthetic, and snoozefest typefaces, these books don't project big "read me and feel better!" energy.

Instead, it's the books with friendly exclamation points that scream *OVER HERE!!! LET ME HELP YOU, SIS!!!* and that are aggressively welcoming, their spines as bright as their pages promise to make you feel. You sort your self-help book collection (because, like the Harry Potter series, you never have a stag self-help book) by color, proud to convey to any and all visitors, *YES, I AM WORKING ON MYSELF.* With a hint of *MAYBE YOU OUGHT TO, TOO, HMMM?*

Really what I'm saying is, it's a shame existentialism didn't have the same PR agent as kale. Just some small smart tweaks could easily take this philosophy out of the ignored outer rim of

Vegas buffets and into shiny dehydrated bags of chips sold for $13.99.

But no, sadly existentialist books stay tucked in dark corners because most of their authors are dead, making their ability to leverage their books a moot point. They can't hook people into their email funnel or sell them into their next Sedona retreat. Their books, unlike those of present-day motivational speakers, aren't elevated business cards, ghostwritten in part to get paid to speak on big stages at multilevel marketing conferences.

An existentialist would have warned me that buying a how-to guide for happiness would turn out to be oxymoronic— because it's copying others instead of living individually that leads to dissatisfaction. They might have told me to just buy Reese's Peanut Butter Cups and call it a day. But sadly, an existentialist wasn't there with me in the student bookstore. So instead, I walked home with an expectationist's ten-step solution for my sadness.

GUIDE ME

I felt monumentally safer with The Guide in my hands. I carried it with me to the dinner table and cuddled it in bed. It rode shotgun in my car and got sand wedged in its cracks at the beach. All my small purses went into early retirement because I'd use only bags spacious enough to fit The Guide. It was like an adult version of a ratty security blanket.

Once I graduated and was back in the safety slash regression of my parents' home, I had nothing but time and no agenda other than to heal.

My ex had done more than break my heart—he shattered my life plan. I had been planning to road-trip to LA with him so I could get my TV writing career going, and he was going to look for a restaurant kitchen to work in. We would have been snuggled in some questionably hygienic comforter at a roadside motel on Route 66 right then, googling apartment rentals as close to the beach as possible. Instead, I was sleeping in my childhood bed above old remnants of hidden Dasani bottles filled with Smirnoff Raspberry, nearly hyperventilating under my Pottery Barn Teen quilt, reading a guide on how to bulldoze my negative thoughts.

This book was the first time that I had heard anyone that resembled me talk about struggling like me. The Guide said she'd been in a dark place and full of worries but had managed to commit to joy and make a miraculous life. This girl had been, literally, in my chestnut Ugg boots. And so I felt safe enough to follow her on a route I'd never tried.

The confusing part was that my family always stressed not to be a follower. If I ever used "But Stephanie's doing it!" I was met with the unoriginal "If Stephanie jumped off the roof, would you jump off the roof, too?"

Now, though, I was told that being a follower was actually an honorable move. If you want what I have, my Guide wrote, do as I do. My Guide revealed that this was her secret strategy for becoming the happiest person in her stratosphere. She had found guides of her own and wanted what they had, so she did what they did. Suddenly, if I applied this code, jumping off roofs with Stephanie seemed less like a bad trip on Ecstasy and more like the smart and spiritual path to ecstasy.

My comfort with my Guide was only strengthened when I learned how to sit and close my eyes and follow her voice while trying to fight urges to itch, pee, or recite the four questions— which is called meditation. Through downloadable MP3 audio tracks on my first-gen iPod, I trusted her voice to lead my thoughts to where they ought to go, which was usually to some place involving bright white light.

It seemed like white light was the visualization equivalent of a Tide to Go stain stick: an easy hack to bleach out dark crap. I learned how to see myself from a ceiling-fan's-eye view and send light down onto me to melt away shame at being sequestered on my parents' couch like a pathetic twat instead of seizing life with the ambitious gusto of a recent college graduate. And I white-lighted my mom for some childhood stuff, because why not. I also imagined white light connecting me to my ex like a glow-in-the-dark extension cord, and I envisioned snipping that cord to rid me of my attachment to him (and to force forgiveness for leaving me high and dry and completely alone and miserable out of nowhere).

Evidence of my Guide's successful methods was the story of how she brought her own ex-boyfriend back. This dream scenario, and often the hottest topic in her live-lecture Q&As, was the one I zipped right to.

According to her, I could forgive by meditating. With meditation, I could energetically dissolve my dysfunctions with my ex by picturing him standing in front of me in a glow of 400-watt white light and repeating "I accept you. I forgive you. Your light reflects my light. Our sidewalk shadows are one."

In his 1961 book, *Thought Reform and the Psychology of Totalism*, psychiatrist Robert Jay Lifton coined the term "thought-terminating cliché"[6] to refer to the simplification of complex human emotions and problems into "brief, highly reductive, definitive-sounding phrases, easily memorized and easily expressed." These critical-thought-crushing catchphrases can hinder deeper introspection, acting as, in Montell's words, a "temporary psychological sedative."

I found that if I repeated these mantras enough while closing my eyes, I could essentially use this imaginary white light as psychological Wite-Out for all the reasons we were ill-fitted. It was incredible. A psychological sedative, indeed. I could have a thought like, *Facebook tells me he's already sleeping with someone new, and that feels like a serrated knife went right through my gut.* And with some bright light here and white rays there, I could bulldoze my thought to *I accept that. I accept him. I forgive him. I hope he's using protection.*

Using more fun lingo, this psychological Wite-Outing can be called "spiritual bypassing," a term popularized by psychologist John Welwood in the 1980s. He described it as using spiritual beliefs and practices to avoid dealing with unresolved emotional issues, psychological wounds, or challenges in relationships. Essentially, it's when people like moi use meditation, affirmations, or positive thinking to ignore or avoid (or bypass) difficult shit rather than face it directly.

It's cathartic to hear all these terms described by psychologists and psychiatrists, because they put words to the ick I felt inside at the time when I was thought-terminating and spiritually-bypassing. But in perfect "cultish" form, I drowned my inside icks by cranking up my faith in this guide's guarantees for happiness.

Meditating the bad away was only half the equation. That was just clearing the slate. Next, it was critical to start filling the slate with crystal-clear mental GIFs of specifically what I wanted, so the universe didn't just throw things willy-nilly my way. Clarity is key so that the cosmos know what to deliver!

The menu of suggested items was pretty straightforward. No fun surprises there. We had the looks, the love, the money, the career, the materials: the ingredients for what our Western society deems the recipe for universal happiness. They were also the very extrinsic values that psychologist Tim Kasser delves into in his book *The High Price of Materialism*—values that share a focus on seeking validation, worth, or fulfillment from *external* sources.

I didn't even flinch at the chapters in the book correlating happiness to the acquisition of these extrinsic values. This so-called materialism is awfully covert. It's not like the book was suggesting that I ask the universe for a fully loaded Maserati, for Pete's sake! But this is where expectationist literature does a freaky bait and switch: it can disguise materialistic goals as personal development, guiding us to prioritize external valida-tion over genuine self-discovery and inner peace.

So it's no wonder that Kasser, in his research on how the pursuit of extrinsic values ultimately corrodes our well-being (spoiler!), developed an "Aspiration Index" that encompassed far more than mere items for which you get emailed a receipt. His index (which I look at like a shopping list) included aspira-tions I was well familiar with: namely those aspirations related to being known, admired, and approved by many people.

I have a friend who couldn't care less about their actual ma-terial items but cares deeply about their actual career label: sci-entist. At the expense of all else—family obligations, their health, stress, time for other hobbies—this person prioritizes chasing after this title of scientist. This is still a material goal. It's an extrinsic value. It's a value that's based on validation and reactions from external sources, versus their own innate desire to actually *do* the science-ing.

Without question, pursuing extrinsic values leads to misery in every conceivable aspect of life. When your self-love is de-rived solely from the validation, opinions, and judgments of others, you become trapped in a cycle of dissatisfaction and discontentment. This relentless pursuit of external validation can erode your sense of self-worth and leave you feeling unfulfilled, no matter how much you achieve or acquire.

You always hear how awful it must feel to be an actor, always auditioning and having your entire career and thus self-worth essentially dictated by gatekeepers' decisions and opinions. But we're all actors in our own lives, and if we live extrinsically motivated lives, we, too, are letting gatekeepers determine our level of happiness. Except these gatekeepers don't work in fancy offices in NYC or LA; they sit in the glow of blue light tap-tap-tapping.

I appreciate how in his book *Lost Connections*, Johann Hari calls extrinsic values "junk values," as opposed to meaningful values: "All this mass-produced fried chicken looks like food, and it appeals to the part of us that evolved to need food; yet it doesn't give us what we need from food—nutrition. Instead, it fills us with toxins."[7] The same is true of materialistic values. Calling yourself a scientist doesn't nourish you; yet, pursuing the title steals your time and energy from consuming nourishment and intrinsic values: family, connection, contentment, purpose, inner peace.

But shhh, I didn't know all this yet! I was still salivating over the taste of the promised good life up ahead of me.

3

. . . .

Flexing Mind Muscles

My Guide said that mentally white-knuckling a wish is called "manifesting," and it's the foundation on which everything else in her playbook is built. Trying to choose happiness without manifesting would be impossible, I learned. It'd be like trying to choose satiety without eating.

My Guide's version of manifesting was to rearrange reality with your mind. It wasn't a passive belief to justify behavior; it was the behavior. *Manifest* was an active verb: bringing things to be (or not be) with your intentions.

Its premise: thoughts become things.

Its promise: you will get whatever you think about.

Its warning: don't think bad things or you'll get them— because of the aforementioned premise and promise.

It never crossed my mind that my Guide wasn't the original creator of these mental magic tricks. Since I had never heard of them, I assumed she thought them up. Probably while healing her reality during a mani-pedi. Now I understand that gurus repurpose others' advice like pop artists do melodies.

I learned about sampling in music when I went through my seminal middle school Eminem phase. At the time there was no one on this planet who could understand me, a thirteen-year-old white, half-Jewish girl with two cats and two parents still married living in the New England suburbs, better than Marshall Mathers. I remember one day I was sitting in the passenger seat of my mom's Jeep Grand Cherokee, staring out the window, when his new song "Stan" came on the radio. Shocked that this deeply dark song about the shortcomings of snail mail would play on the same family-friendly FM station that plays Mandy Moore's "Candy," I perked up. But as the song kept going, with Dido singing "My tea's gone cold . . . ," my boy Eminem's voice never came on. I was so confused. This was the first time I experienced music sampling.

Sampling is when a rhythm, melody, riff, or hook from one song is used in a brand-new song. In the music biz, sampling is commonplace. It's fun, creative, accepted, and respectful. It's also acknowledged, embraced, and admitted outwardly. For listeners, it's also really fun when 50 percent of the time, after we hear those "duh duh duh duth, duh duh duh duh, duh duh duh duh dnernernernra," we're right that it's "All Summer Long" by Kid Rock and not "Sweet Home Alabama" or "Werewolves of London"!

But I hadn't realized that sampling in the self-help industry is commonplace, too. Even starting with the term itself—self-help.

In 1859, a Scottish writer and progressive reformist named Samuel Smiles published a book. Cool, lots of people publish books. But Smiles's book wasn't an ordinary book. It was the Penicillin of Books because it became one of those unintentional inventions like penicillin, Botox, and Viagra. In Smiles's case, it was a book genre that he invented: *Self-Help.*

(That's the name of the book.)

(And the genre.)

Obviously, you can find dusty older versions of self-help writings by the Greeks, Buddhists, Jews, and all sorts of age-old scribes. But as Beth Blum, an assistant professor of English at Harvard specializing in modernist and contemporary litera-ture, said in an interview on the podcast *Writ Large*, "It's use-ful to differentiate between the history of conduct literature and the rise of the self-help industry proper, which I think really hinges on Samuel Smiles in the publication of his book in the context of self culture surrounding that."[1]

This was totally one of those "right time, right place" kinds of books, because *Self-Help* came out when work conditions were extremely poor and people were wishing for ways to im-prove their individual circumstances and find more happiness. "Many people found themselves stuck working long hours in factories, often in miserable conditions," said Blum. "People were being treated no better than the machines they operated. [Smiles] saw that there was a need for sources who could in-spire and rouse working-class individuals to kind of band to-gether and to educate themselves."

Smiles was said to later regret his book's title because many people, unfortunately, misunderstood his intentions. Critics criticized (because what else do critics do?) *Self-Help* for pro-moting selfishness, as in *Help Only Yourself.* While I can see where they were coming from, Smiles meant it like, *Look! You don't need to sit on your arse all day waiting for help. You can help* yourself! Even more, he hoped that by one helping one's own self, the collective selves would be improved as well, just like that "rising tide lifting all boats" thing.

Essentially, Smiles wanted to help regular ol' folks (men) not to feel limited by their natural-born (white privilege) circumstances. He did this by pairing tangible tough-love advice with real success stories of chemists, linguists, and other people who worked hard, persevered in overcoming adversity, and, like your grandparents, walked eight miles in the snow—barefoot—just to learn to read at the town school.

I believe his intention was to convey that we're now creating machines and learning how to do impressive things, but also an understanding that our mind is a machine, too. So let's use it! Let's flex our mind muscle. And I think this was pretty groundbreaking information for people. "His wish in writing it," journalist Will Storr writes in *Selfie*, "was 'to stimulate youths to apply themselves diligently and to the right pursuits—sparing neither labour, pains, nor self-denial in prosecuting them—and to rely upon their own efforts in life, rather than depend upon the help or patronage of others.'"[2]

"He would probably have been horrified to walk into a modern bookshop and see an entire section of self-help books, large numbers of which seem to promise an entirely new life just by reading them," writes journalist Steve Shipside. "He was keenly aware of the difference between theorising about life and experiencing it first hand and was at pains to emphasize that *Self-Help* was a collection of illustrations from life rather than a distillation, a short cut, a magic bullet,"[3] which is perhaps why you won't find Smiles's original *Self-Help* book at airport bookstores where they hawk life-hack books in a one-to-one ratio with C-shape neck pillows.

Smiles's *Self-Help* explosion in industrial Europe was stirring up brain waves in corners of quaint New England.

In my quaint bedroom in Connecticut in 2011, manifestation was completely new to me. Same as it was for folks in the mid-1800s, when it was called New Thought.

Not to be confused with New Age (the yoga, meditation, and spiritual movement that spread like patchouli incense throughout the Western world in the 1970s), New Thought (or the New Thought movement) is named because of many new . . . thoughts . . . people started embracing in the early nineteenth century.

In comparison with the newer ones, the old thoughts were rooted in Calvinism, which was the reigning faith for over two hundred years when the first settlers arrived on the land that would eventually become part of the United States. Calvinism was a rigid, oppressive religion that forbade questioning God, believing in science, thinking for yourself, and showing emotion. Calvinists thought that God's admission tickets to heaven had nothing to do whatsoever with one's earthly actions, so you had no control over your own destiny and were devoid of any influence in shaping your ultimate fate.

But then came the New Thought movement, which believed, quite literally, the complete opposite. It was like when you quit being vegan by becoming a full-blown carnivore instead of just phasing some fish back into your diet. There was no fish for these former Calvinists. These people went ham. Whole hog. New Thought taught that each person had a "God within," and they could tap into this power through positive thinking to create the life they desired.

New Thought popped up in Portland, Maine, where a clockmaker named Phineas Parkhurst Quimby became fascinated with faith healing.

Believe it or not, faith healers' successes were hit-or-miss.

As author Barbara Ehrenreich writes in *Bright-Sided*, "In

New Thought, illness was a disturbance in an otherwise perfect Mind and could be cured through the Mind alone. Sadly, the strictly mental approach did not seem to work with infectious diseases—such as diphtheria, scarlet fever, typhus, tuberculosis, and cholera—that ravaged America until the introduction of public sanitary measures at the end of the nineteenth century."[4]

Soon it would pick up steam when William James, the famed founder of American psychology, dubbed it the "mind-cure movement," and it went more mainstream. It would also sprout offshoots like when Frances Lord, a Christian Scientist, published the "prosperity gospel," instructions on how to cure the mental bonds of poverty. The acceleration of "mind muscling" continues to expand and offshoot even today. It's like when cauliflower realized it could be pizza and then inserted itself into rice, crackers, pretzels, and lord knows what's next: it seems to have picked up on the power of belief.

When not making clocks, this guy Quimby doodled metaphysical musings in his journals. He became fervently convinced that other patients around town were feeling better only because *they believed in* their healer's magical powers. (As opposed to the healer having actual healing powers—known today as a form of placebo effect.)

My nonofficial records imagine a Quimby diary entry might've gone something like this:

Dear Diary, I'm sorry it's taken me so long to write to you again. I would say I lost track of time, but you'd see right through me. Anyway, I don't think it's Preacher Herbert that helped little Agnes's measles and Miss Fannie's smallpox. I really think it was their belief in Preacher Herbert's healing powers. "The cure is not in the medicine but in the confidence of the doctor or me-dium." So I have decided to put clock-making on hold and open my own healing practice where I will sit face-to-face with my patients and get them to believe that their ailments have originated in their minds. Wish me luck! Love, Phineas. PS: I promise I'll write again soon. PPS: I can't wait to prove my "talking cure" is legit.

Unsurprisingly, Quimby's "Why cannot I cure myself?" road to self-healing was awfully appealing—who in their right mind wouldn't want the ability to wish away a UTI? As Storr writes in *Selfie*, "In this magical time of invisible forces such as the electric light and the telegraph there developed a craze for faith healing. The key to the cure—to happiness, to health, to salvation—lay within them. All they had to do was *believe*."[5]

It was also notably a complete 180 from fearing a spiteful, hostile jerk of a Calvinist god who once disempowered all citizens by considering rest and relaxation a sin. Because New Thought's higher power was a loving mind-spirit blend who said, "Sin no more!"

Instead, as Ehrenreich writes in *Bright-Sided*, "If [sin] existed at all, it was an 'error,' as was disease, because if everything was Spirit or Mind or God, everything was actually perfect. The trick, for humans, was to access the boundless power of Spirit and thus exercise control over the physical world."[6]

It was like people had finally moved out of their superstrict home with rules and manners and a mom who snooped her way through every crevasse in their room while they were in school and then they got to college and went buck wild on the Adderall they managed to hide from their mom! Except these former Calvinists' buck wild was feeling free to use their own thoughts to control the physical world, and it was spectacular.

This concept soon picked up steam when William James dubbed it "the religion of healthy-mindedness" in his book *The Varieties of Religious Experience*. That took mind-curing mainstream. Sadly for James, but fortunately for Quimby, James had terribly fragile health from the jump. After suffering from pain, exhaustion, and invalidism to the point of contemplating suicide, poor James was "mind-cured" by a disciple of Quimby's. Though as a psychologist James was a man of science, James was also a philosopher, a man of spirit, so he leaned on his anecdotal experience of being healed to accept New Thought "woo-woo" as legit. In *The Varieties of Religious Experience*, James writes:

> One hears of the "Gospel of Relaxation," of the "Don't Worry Movement" [later rebranded by Disney as the "Hakuna Matata Movement"], of people who repeat to themselves, "Youth, health, vigor!" when dressing in the morning as their motto for the day. Complaints of the weather are getting to be forbidden in many households; and more and **more people are recognizing it to be bad form to speak of disagreeable sensations** or to make much of the ordinary inconveniences and ailments of life.[7] (boldface emphasis mine)

When one reads the above excerpt, one may think this sounds like the early seeds of what we call toxic positivity today. (Or *new* New Thought? More on this later.) People started fearing their thoughts, becoming paranoid that letting one negative thought or even a mild complaint about "ordinary inconveniences" like the weather would blow their whole life up! And bring rain on their wedding day! Indeed, this Hakuna Matata problem-free philosophy rested completely on one's ability to *have only positive thoughts for the rest of your days*, which means *never having negative thoughts for the rest of your days*, which creates *endlessly exhausting self-monitoring and paranoia for the rest of your days*, which in a sense sounds even worse than having some worries. Perhaps what should've been proposed here was "a problem-lite philosophy," where one aims to walk down life on the sunny side of the street but is also free to bitch about the rain.

Mary Baker Eddy, a follower of Phineas Quimby, was deeply influenced by his teachings on the power of positive thinking and mental healing. She founded the Christian Science movement, which emphasized these principles and promoted spiritual healing through prayer and affirmation. Eddy authored the seminal work *Science and Health with Key to the Scriptures* and established the Church of Christ, Scientist.

While Eddy's teachings resonated with many seeking spiritual and physical healing, the term "prosperity gospel" didn't emerge until later. This term became popularized in the mid-twentieth century to describe a theological emphasis on material blessings and financial prosperity within certain branches of Christianity. Early proponents of prosperity teachings included figures like E. W. Kenyon and Oral Roberts.

In the broader context of New Thought–inspired literature, Wallace D. Wattles's book *The Science of Getting Rich* offers insights into the power of thought and visualization in achieving success. While not directly tied to Christian Science or the prosperity gospel, Wattles's work contributed to the burgeoning self-help movement of its time.

It was in 1937 when Napoleon Hill, a nobody turned drifter turned famous self-help author, told everyone to think and grow rich. His bestseller of the same name is based on the premise that the magical wealth-generating ideas he revealed therein come from his rich pal, the American steel magnate Andrew Carnegie, who urged Hill—Moses and the Ten Commandments style—that he *must* share them with the world. Except there is zero proof from anyone, including from Carnegie's own biographer, David Nasaw, that Carnegie even knew Hill existed, let alone entrusted him with his "13 steps to riches," which include, my favorite, number 10: Use the power of your sexual energy to fuel your desire and drive. Regardless of Hill's integrity, his methods clearly worked, because he thought and grew very, *very* rich. His book was woo-woo in many of its principles but was marketed as a serious business strategy.

Not much later, in 1952, a Protestant minister named Norman Vincent Peale said he "owed Hill a debt of gratitude for his writings," which helped Peale publish *The Power of Positive Thinking*. Weaving in his religious undertones, Peale once again remixed the law of attraction and made wealth holy.

In 1976, a woman named Louise Hay self-published a pamphlet called *Heal Your Body*, which documented how she had cured her incurable vaginal cancer by releasing resentful thoughts about the childhood sexual assault she had endured. In *You Can Heal Your Life*, her little pamphlet turned book, which sold well over 35 million copies, she paired nearly every type of bodily ailment with an affirmation to heal the ailment's probable metaphysical cause.

"I've learned that for every condition in our lives," Hay writes in *Heal Your Body*, "there's a need for it. Otherwise, we wouldn't have it. The symptom is only an outer effect. We must go within to dissolve the mental cause." For example, she writes that the probable cause for canker sores, a condition that I get cursed with way too frequently, is "festering words held back by the lips." Her suggested new thought pattern is "I create only joyful experiences in my loving world." (It's amazing how setting an hourly alarm on my phone with that affirmation plus an entire container of canker sore goo and rest help calm the sores on my tongue that seem to pop up when my immune system is compromised.)

Next in the evolution of creating reality with our craniums, in 2006 Oprah Winfrey took a break from gifting free cars to audience members to bequeath them with something else—a secret. This secret was yet *another* remix of the OG New Thought, but this time it was presented not in book form (that would come later) but rather in a fancy documentary, with an alluring Australian accent to boot. The filmmaker, Rhonda Byrne, branded the law of attraction, or LOA, as a majestic ancient secret that we viewers should feel relieved to *finally* be learning. That secret? Positive thoughts attract positive experiences, and negative thoughts attract negative experiences. *Shhhhhh.*

Byrne's version of the LOA featured a more scientific bent than others, dropping terms like "vibrations" and leaning heavily on the "law" concept, as if it's akin to the law of gravity. (It isn't.) "Remember that you are like a magnet, attracting everything to you," Byrne's voice-over says melodically. "Like all the laws of nature, the law of attraction is immutable; no one is above it or excluded from it. It is impersonal, and operates on all of us equally—on every subject, and on every single thought."

To show the equality of the law, the film featured many a talking-head figure, from chiropractors to marketing experts to metaphysicians, all telling us in their warm (mostly white and grandfatherly) tone that the cause for everything in our life (poverty, illness, belly fat, an unmade bed) is not sometimes, but *always* our thoughts. *Always.* And so, the documentary/ book says, "this secret is the secret to everything—the secret to

unlimited joy, health, money, relationships, love, youth: everything you have ever wanted."[8]

What likely fostered *The Secret*'s massive success (besides
Oprah's public loyalty and Byrne's positive thoughts, of course)
was that it blended New Agey (but old thoughty) thinking with
modern materialism.

We viewers are told the LOA is "like having the universe as
your catalog," and they use fancy cars, token parking spots,
oversize houses, and straight-up wads of cash as examples of
the catalog offerings. The cost? Your imagination! "If you're
imagining in your mind that you have the brand new car, the
money that you need, finding the soul mate . . . if you're imagining what that looks like, you're emitting that frequency. . . .
Your thoughts are sending out that magnetic signal that is
drawing the parallel back to you."[9] In other words, *The Secret*
shouts at us: YOU WILL ATTRACT IT!

The Secret catapulted the law of attraction into the zeit-
geist. LOA wasn't just a pseudoscientific law or a smartly marketed get-rich "secret" anymore. It was now a verb, a thing you
do. You attract. You vibrate. You manifest. I mean, if you're
desperate enough, you take the LOA as absolute fact and *then*
you manifest.

This is exactly what I did as I sat in my teenage bedroom in
between a dusty, deflated blue workout ball and a small wooden
Ethan Allen nightstand with one tiny drawer overstuffed with
printed-out critically important AIM conversations from yes-
teryear. I dove into what I thought was fresh advice from a
spunky and bright twentysomething, when it was really, as I
know now, kind of kooky unsubstantiated ideas passed down
from the journal of a nineteenth-century clockmaker.

I sped-read paragraphs faster than the narrow illumination
of my book light could keep up with. (So I had to keep re-

clamping the light to accommodate my rapid page-turning. Pro tip: headlamp.)

What I believe, I receive?! I can be a magnet for what I desire?! Everything that I have now was once a thought that I thought? And to get more, I have to clear thoughts that are limiting my ability to think about what I want? What if it doesn't work? Do I just try harder until it does? Quiet! Don't think that way!

In my desperation and optimism, I had to believe that the law of attraction was real. Twenty-two years of hearing a very respectable little man with a soft coaster on his head stand on a platform and tell me that Moses lifted a stick and turned the Red Sea into a one-way road out of Dodge, and I'm thinking, *Meh, I'm not so sure.* But twenty-four minutes of reading a paperback by a stranger with pretty hair telling me that by bait-and-switching my thoughts—*all* of them—from negativity to positivity, I can manifest like a goddamn genie, and I'm like, *Sounds about right.* (And the first guy could play a ram's horn like a clarinet!)

But at the time, I needed something. A crutch. A protocol. A system. All of the above. And since I'd already spent the majority of my time stuck in my head, I figured I might as well use the law of attraction to win my guy back.

Miraculously, after about a month of feverishly forgiving and white-lighting, I completed my first manifestation. It played out like this:

First, I meditated to get my energy clean.

Then I dialed his number and sent thoughts of love while it rang.

"Hello?" he said when he picked up.

"Hi, how are you?" I replied.

"Good, what about you?"

"I'm good. I've been really working on myself and I've really changed. I'm so sorry for how I used to be. I was so caught up in fear and limit—"

"OK."

"Well, I've been thinking. Can we meet up? Maybe find somewhere halfway," I nervously threw out there, ready to add "but closer to you!" if needed.

"Why?"

"It'd just be nice to have some closure."

"Closure?" he asked.

I am both desperate and completely self-improved, I thought. "I'd really like to find peace with you face-to-face" is what I said.

Silence is what I heard.

"You promised you'd give me a chance to work on myself," I now said out loud, my voice starting to break.

Then my inner guide led me to remind him, "If it weren't for my grandma gifting you her bright red, dinged-up 1997 red Ford Probe with the cool pop-up headlights when she moved into her nursing home, you wouldn't even have a car at all!" He finally, begrudgingly, agreed to meet me. I couldn't believe it. Manifest complete. Boom! Magic.

On my way to our miraculous meetup, I listened to a playlist of high-vibe songs my Guide had gifted to me in exchange for my email address.

When my ex climbed out of my grandma's car in the parking lot and immediately started sucking down a cigarette, I tried to hide my disgust that he'd not only picked up this one habit I abhor (and had watched him/helped him/forced him to quit) but was doing it in my face as a stinky, Marlboro Light fuck-you. With some deep inhales and exhales, and lots of sending of white light and love from my heart to his, I felt my betrayal evaporate like leftover beer in the cans I saw cluttering the backseat of my baba's car.

By my taking only two meditation breaks and doing a lot of blabbering inner self-talk, my thoughts and his tongue became my reality at this meeting. (We made out.)

A few hours after parting ways, my phone rang.

"Hey," he said.

"Hey!"

"It was really good seeing you today . . ."

And just like I envisioned, we were back in the running! I was elated. And a full convert to the LOA.

It had worked: I had manifested us back together—just like my guru did with her ex! We stayed together for a short time— the exact length of time I was able to suppress negative thoughts, acting fearfully, or being myself.

But even though that relationship obviously didn't last, I had proof of the efficacy of these magical mental-gymnastic moves, which was thrilling. But now I didn't know what to do with my superpower: The pommel horse? Uneven bars? Balance beam?

I was a freshly minted adult with virtually no clue where to really start this "life" thing.

Had I been reading existentialism at the time, I'd have been able to articulate that the freaked-out feeling I was experiencing was simply the seasonal allergies of normal life transition. The predictable paralysis from the world being my freshly polished oyster.

But I wasn't reading existentialism at the time. I was reading self-help, the cheerleaders of the Aspiration Index of extrinsic values. And so it was self-help that guided me on to a stuffed rush-hour subway car on the 6 train and then to an old apartment building in the East Village for a lecture on cocreating with the universe.

4

. . . .

All About the Benjamin (Franklin)

After I pressed an intercom button and heard a cheerful "Come on up, babe!" I trudged up four flights of crappy narrow stairs that led to a hidden gem of a yoga studio with polished hard-wood floors, a wall of exposed brick, soft lighting, and about fifty other women who looked just like me. In the front of the room, in between two fiddle-leaf figs, sat my Guide in a jewel-toned kaftan, chitchatting, sipping Smartwater, and radiating like she chose the crap out of happiness that day. This wasn't the first time I'd seen her speak (or what she called "lecturing," because it sounds more worthy of charging big bucks), but it was certainly the most intimate.

Somewhere between inhaling through my nose and exhal-ing through my mouth, I took in the room. I was in a sea of meditating women like myself. All of us spending our precious postwork hours hustling, not to get served a New Zealand sauv blanc in a crowded bar, but to get served secrets to happy living by a charismatic woman. As instructed, we rested our hands lightly on our crossed legs with our open palms facing up. Even though palms face down felt more natural, I kept mine flipped, anticipating that I'd be able to grasp her contagious magnetism.

When the guided meditation ended, we were instructed to slowly open our eyes.

"Now that's a high better than coke, am I right, ladies?"

As the easiest audience ever laughed at my Guide's joke, I felt a chill come over me. In that moment, a voice seemed to be whisper-shouting to me, *This. This is what you're meant to do.*

I felt confused about what that voice meant, because I certainly did not want to be teaching spirituality or wearing a kaftan. So I squeezed my eyes tightly and dug really deep—I mean, let the universe float some thoughts my way. I knew I wanted to be happy. And I knew I was not that—not yet. I saw my Guide was happy. And I saw a flyer that said next week she was hosting a workshop called "How to Manifest an Abundant Business." I sent her my RSVP vibe and prayed this week would fly by.

Being a business owner was never a career path I'd entertained. But looking at my glowy Guide in the front of the yoga room talking about making money from her yoga pants and overflowing in abundance from doing purpose-driven work, I'll admit that I felt pretty . . . spoken to. And it seemed that perhaps, maybe, probably, if I tilted my head and squinted with willingness to look at it a certain way, the universe was sending me blatant guidance I'd be remiss to miss. The ball was in my court to muster up the courage to collaborate with the universe and once again heed the call.

This, I now understand, was when girlbossing blended with the prosperity gospel. I drank the smoothie.

Phrases I'd read like "finding your true purpose" seemed empowering and profound but subtly reinforced the idea that happiness and fulfillment are contingent on external achieve-ments—our purpose is strangely always something that makes money and looks impressive to our old high school Facebook friends.

Looking back on this now, in the mid 2020s, I feel like I'm telling you about a rotary phone. Today we are constantly get-ting calls about things we need to do and achieve: *Make money while you breastfeed! Work part-time but make a full-time in-come! Turn your purpose into profit!* (No offense, but at this point, I kind of judge you if you *haven't* shamefully tried an MLM.)

It was almost as if my Guide was telling us about the birds and the bees; she stated that when we find our purpose, team up with the energy of the universe, and serve people with love, then success and happiness inevitably await us. Expectationism.

After attending her make-bank-in-yoga-clothes workshop, I was committed to following the light. And that night, reaching for my probiotics beneath the glow of my refrigerator light, it hit me that I could apply my love of writing and performing comedy to my healthy vegan cooking chops, which I'd learned to heal my debilitating digestive problems. And boom! My pur-suit to be "Rachael Ray meets Ellen DeGeneres" was born, and my brand name, PartyInMyPlants.com, was purchased.

Fortunately, my timing couldn't have been more ideal (thanks, universe), because it was suddenly easier than ever be-fore in history to *see what they have, so I could do what they do.* Social media, namely YouTube and the brand-new photo-focused app Instagram, shocked us by gifting us something we never knew we always wanted: the opportunity to literally fol-low the leader—and/or/also aspire to be a leader to follow. Be-fore Instagram, we'd have to read about our guides in magazines? Or find a *60 Minutes* segment to DVR?

But on social media, I discovered that my Guide had her guides, and they had *their* guides, and it was like the blind leading the blind and collecting the desperate (me) along the way.

Anytime I felt lost, I had some helpful book to bring me back to my hustle mentality. And when I felt sad, I had guides to remind me to practice gratitude and block all low-vibe thoughts. I had Instagram accounts to help me arrange my items to allow the flow of happiness, YouTube videos for organizing my time, online courses on writing catchy social media posts, and coaches enlisted to help me lose ten pounds for TV by training my subconscious to want to be thin. Ne'er a moment passed that I wasn't in manifesting mode. I was not only bulldozing my thoughts, just like my first guidebook had promised, but I was bulldozing my way to the top at lightning speed. (And very little sleep.) I was moving so fast and sleeping so little that the minuscule part of me that stomped and screamed, *Stop! Stop! You aren't happy!* had no chance of being heard over Queen's "We Are the Champions," which was soundtracking my success montage.

My personality and my brand were so seamlessly intertwined and so awesomely authentic that at my wedding, my dad incorporated Party in My Plants' success story into his wedding toast. Film crews came to my home to shoot inspiring segments about me being a "shining example of a female entrepreneur." I was chosen to collaborate on an international edutational commercial series that ended with me dancing alongside a simulated avocado. My podcast got rave reviews, my speaking calendar filled up, and I manifested a dream comedy-cookbook deal from my dream publisher with a dream editor with my face on the front and my words inside.

I became a "regular guest on *Dr. Oz*," a title I, of course, added to enhance every conversation, like salt in a recipe. I married a perfect (for me) husband, and we got an adorable (to everyone) goldendoodle. We bought a house! My book debuted on *Good Morning America*, and my face was plastered on a big screen in Times Square! I was thirty and had achieved all I'd ever pursued. The Guide had worked to a T.

One afternoon, as I was crossing Fifth Avenue in Manhattan playing some inspirational podcast in my ears, I walked right into Tiffer, a kinda friend from college. He was as friendly and charming as I'd remembered, and he instantly gave me a warm hello and a hug. When he pulled back, he repeated many of my accolades to me. He referenced my book, TV appearances, and large social media following. Then he introduced me to the colleague he was walking with.

"This is Talia," Tiffer told him. "She's famous!"

I used to dream of the f-word. I'd imagine going places and being known. Getting asked back to my high school as a noteworthy alumna and having the whole town come out in awe. Standing room only in our auditorium.

So now, standing on the street, hearing someone whose admiration should've been a 10 out of 10 call me "famous," I expected to feel IT.

Feel what? I don't know, but IT. I figured I'd know IT when I felt IT. But I didn't. I had successfully followed the advice "If you want what she has, do what she does," and had done what she did, but I didn't have the happiness that she said she had.

I felt like I was at that water-shooting game at a carnival and I'd focused superhard and made the strong flow of water from the stationary water gun hit the bull's-eye, but when it did, I was blank. Why wasn't I more . . . enthused?

My Guide was all "Fake it until you make it," but never explained when I could stop faking. So I'd made it from faking it, but now I felt like a phony who'd made it.

Worst of all, there wasn't a troubleshooting page in The Guide. There was no "PS: Here's what to do after you've fixed yourself and manifested your dreams and still aren't happy."

So, to feel better, I did all the things. I scrolled through my podcast reviews to force feelings of gratitude.

I went for a run to generate positive energy.

You surpassed every goal you set! I reminded myself. *Others have vision boards with your achievements Elmer's-glued to them. What more could you possibly need to feel good? You are soooo self-sabotaging right now. Get out of your own way, sis!*

I found old photos of former pathetic Talia to contrast with present-day me. (And I threw in a quick comparison with my ex's totally less cool wife for an extra side of fries.)

I wasn't happy from all the things that were supposed to make me happy.

Maybe I had low blood sugar. I ate a banana. Still unenthused. I confirmed mercury was not in retrograde, nor was my monthly moon cycle about to come. I was still unenthused.

Have you ever beaten yourself up for being apathetic? It's painfully paradoxical to be more riled up about not being riled up than about actually being riled up. But logic is no deterrence to feelings. And I started to feel . . . broken.

"Remember when you wanted everything you have now," I told myself, recalling something I'd read somewhere that was supposed to be helpful for making your guilt spark gratitude.

I time-traveled back to when I wanted everything I now had. I saw myself standing in the kitchen of my college apartment whacking open a coconut. This is a thing one did back in 2009 when one wanted to enjoy the health benefits of drinking pure coconut water before one could get cartons of it at gas stations. So I had my coconut resting on my linoleum countertop, and in between chops with an old cleaver I'd borrowed from my parents, who previously used it to perform surgery on our Thanksgiving turkeys, I was watching The Dr. Oz Show, a cozy and cheerful daytime talk program featuring a handsome surgeon next door who sometimes showed up in scrubs and other times emerged in business casual hawking healthy-living hacks.

The earliest days of the show were known, affectionately to some, as his era of poop smears and colon tunnels, which coincidentally lined up with my era of poop tests and colon constipation. While Dr. Mehmet Oz demonstrated how to interpret our bowel movements in the toilet like tarot cards, and crawled through a kids' play tunnel disguised as a colon to show the wonder that is fiber, I'd looked around my kitchen with my fibrous flaxseeds and soaked nuts. I'd watch his star guests with their shiny hair and effervescent joy teach him about the shocking top four erogenous zones or how to Zumba off the weight or a groundbreaking new way to eat pomegranates. And since I was already majoring in television and spending my days producing and writing video content, I would think how bananas it would be if I were to ever get to green-smoothie cheers with Mehmet on that stage. Pipe-dream status. (Pre–gun wielding, political-crisis Mehmet.)

Seven years later, I'm on that stage, with the humongous cameras and bright lights, and shiny hair. On one part of the set, an art designer is putting the finishing touches on a hibiscus tea display already cued up with a matching floral design taking over the massive screen behind it. Around me are a couple of hundred middle-aged women seated with eager anticipation, all wearing their approved "audience attire" with no prints or logos. The crowd comedian was doing one of his tried-and-tested (and tired) pep-rally bits, getting those women giddy in

their seats—as if Mehmet holding hands and making meaningful eye contact with some lucky audience members wasn't elec-
trifying enough.

A producer shouts something, which clears all the extra
hands off the stage, and the ladies in the crowd quiet down, and
cameramen on dollies roll into position. Dr. Oz starts the segment with his warm, word-blending doctor voice most of us
could recognize anywhere: "... Here to show us how, author of
Party in Your Plants and host of *The Party in My Plants* podcast, Talia Pollock!"

He said my name right this time! I think, as I reflexively
transform into what a mentor once called my "performance
voice," a high-pitched, spirited tone that's as lively as my hands
are. "Dr. Oz loves your energy," a producer counseled me earlier when I was backstage in the greenroom, trying to carefully
memorize the key health benefits of hibiscus. With a wink and
a slight whisper, she then said, "We book you for your personality!"

Even though "that stuff is less important," I nail my lines,
hit my marks, and remember that crushlike chemistry I love
sharing, very publicly, with Oz. Our segment ends, and we
smile for some quick shots for social media. I hear a girl behind
us whisper to her friend, "She's so pretty," and I know she's
talking about me. Dr. Oz is rushed over to stage right, where
his next guest, an expert on so-and-so, is waiting, probably
mentally rehearsing his lines about this and that, hoping his
good performance will give him an off-screen boost in clout,
book sales, or at the very least, dopamine.

As I walk off the set, I take in a panoramic view of this
moment—it was a dream so marvelously come true that it
should be in the manifestation hall of fame. And some self-help
gurus' testimonial pages.

But instead of the overwhelming happiness I expect to feel, what I'm overcome with is emptiness.

Warm tears snapped me back into the present, six years later, on my couch. I opened my eyes and asked myself, *Why am I crying?*

Because of apathy, I responded.

Who feels sad about not feeling happy? I judged.

Someone who believes that happiness is a choice, I replied, knowing well enough that I, "someone," was failing at making myself happy.

This is the acute danger of expectationist literature. If we're diligent and trusting readers of self-improvement, we'll *do what they do* because we believe we *want what they have* because they tell us, *Hey, if you want what I have, you've gotta do what I do.*

But we will usually not feel as good as they tell us we should expect to feel.

Because if you've ever heard a friend tell you "the funniest story ever!" you already know how expectations ruin everything.

BULLOCK CARTS AND BEN FRANKLIN

We have a running joke (which is really just a truth told in a singsong tone) in my household that Jesse doesn't read books. Again, it's not so much a joke as it is a very accurate fact. But it's OK, because every time we go on vacation, I bring enough books for both of us plus every other passenger on the plane. And each flight attendant. And their pets.

On our honeymoon years ago, I told my brand-new husband it was "buy-a-book time." I wanted to read together on parallel loungers like an idyllic Mr. and Mrs. He did a little research and wound up with the extra-thick, 443-page-book

Sapiens by Yuval Noah Harari, which conveniently doubles as a kettlebell. I know that because I carried the kettlebell of a book with me on every trip, beach day, or long weekend for the next two years, as he read it in three-page chunks before burning out.

It seemed like Jesse thought reading a great book is like eating when pregnant: a thing you do for two. So he'd read something brilliant and tap me with a "Babe! Babe!" until I put down my book and listened. That's how I second-handed *Sapiens*-ed.

"The most important finding of all," he read aloud one day, "is that happiness does not really depend on objective conditions of either wealth, health, or even community. Rather, it depends on the correlation between objective conditions and subjective expectations." He looked up to ensure I was still listening, which I was struggling to do, as my brain subconsciously tuned out when it heard words that triggered MATH!

"All he's saying," Jesse translated, "is we can only be happy when we meet our expectations. The mismatch between expectations and reality creates unhappiness."

He picked up *Sapiens* again. "If you want a bullock-cart," he continued reading, "and you get a bullock-cart, you are content. If you want a brand-new Ferrari and get only a second-hand Fiat, you feel deprived." He closed the book with his finger between the pages to save his place. "I imagine the distance between the expectation and the reality grows in proportion to the distress."

"The greater the gappy, the more unhappy," I contributed, because I turn everything into a jingle. And because I was drinking a chilled bottle of Wölffer hard cider.

It's for this reason that I no longer Instagram-stalk a hotel in advance of a vacation. (Also because the number of times

I've been let down by a hotel room would be shameful to admit.) Expectations are the killer of joy. Without them, we can all live a much freer life.

But ignoring expectations takes willful effort. They're everywhere! Expectations are in performative social media posts where beauty influencers portray themselves as happy because of the lipstick they wear, or minimalist YouTube gurus show their utter joy over owning only one bowl. Expectations are, of course, abundant in self-help content, where motivational speakers or TikTok therapists explain how their simple seven-point process made them happy, so it should unquestionably make us happy, too. Expectations are abundant in cultural storytelling, showing a happy family at the Thanksgiving table, college being a peak life experience, and even, ew, skiing being *comfortable.*

Expectations are the proverbial carrots dangling in front of our noses. We get hooked by anticipation—we can be easily seduced by the promise of future satisfaction. We're encouraged to look ahead. The present is simply a rest stop on the way to a future point of joy. We're convinced that happiness is like a senior citizen's movie-ticket discount: a place we arrive and then stay in forever.

And when things—objects, achievements, or people—inevitably do not make us feel the level of happiness we expect, it's our fault. User error. In this sense, our lack of happiness is a ubiquitous source of unhappiness. Around and around the un-merry-go-round we go.

I had aways assumed we were hardwired to desire happiness and to make our pursuit of it the main point of our existence. I hadn't stopped to think about *why* that was. I guess I assumed that white-knuckling ourselves to be happy is an ingrained human instinct, like how we instinctively pull our hands away from hot things because that hurts, and how we innately feel the biological drive to humpty-dumpty to procreate.

Well, I learned it isn't human nature to desire happiness. It's American nature. And for that, we have Benjamin Franklin to thank.

What failed to hit the history textbooks I was forced to read growing up was that Ben didn't just invent bifocals and libraries and firefighters and then wind up on our $100 bills and as the star of Puff Daddy's 1996 smash-hit rap anthem "It's All About the Benjamins." Ben invented the pursuit of happiness that has become our nation's brand.

If America had a personal-brand website, the mission statement would probably read something like, *America, Land of the Free, Home of the Bottomless Brunch*, and the company's values would be some rendition of *Empowering Mavericks, Fueling Breakthroughs, Fostering Dreams of Going Viral*, and the About page would absolutely have Ben's story in all its glory, with ideally an updated and photoshopped headshot.

In fact, though we do consider, of course, our Declaration of Independence and Constitution our nation's About page(s), it is really Ben's own autobiography, modestly titled *The Autobiography*, that first put into print the American dream (though that term wasn't coined until later), complete with the rags-to-riches fairy tale and all. Ben's own story *was* a rags-to-riches tale. He was, as Jess McHugh writes in *Americanon*, "self-made not only in the sense that he came from no inheritance and built a fortune but also in that he invented and reinvented himself by sheer force of will."[1]

As a prolific writer (quite conveniently, he owned the main printing press in Philadelphia), he imprinted his own success story into the collective ethos, giving bold advice as to how to achieve the would-be-dubbed American dream like it ain't no thang (not a direct quote).

Ben's lifelong outward obsession with happiness and success, which he interlinked, is said to be what inspired Thomas Jefferson to add it to the preamble of the Declaration of Independence in 1776. After all, documentarian Ken Burns refers to Ben as "America's first happiness professor." Apparently, Ben was able to get TJ so hyped about happiness that he actually wove it into the Declaration in about five other places, all of which got vetoed by the rest of the founding fathers. So we know its reference mainly from it being listed as among our unalienable rights: life, liberty, and the pursuit of happiness.

Writing that into our country's mission statement was akin to our forefathers blowing a foghorn at the start of a race. *On your mark, get set, GO! Pursue! Pursue! Pursue the Happiness!* Which might have been a good thing if happiness was like an apple or something, where we could run to the local farmer or climb a tree and capture it for ourselves. But it isn't, so people, rightly, were instantly confused.

So confused, in fact, that they got pissed. Not long after the Declaration debuted, the Constitution was signed, the overturned carriages from the overly zealous partygoers were right side up, and the Bud Light cans from the epic first Fourth of July celebration were swept away, many freshly minted Americans were like, *Umm, where's our happiness at?* They trepidatiously turned to their neighbors to inquire if they were also experiencing a hard time accessing this new happiness. Like, *Hey, did you get today's Wordle? And also, do you have your happiness?*

Most of them did not.

So, hundreds of unhappy people blamed the government, because they believed their happiness was now protected by law, and *Umm, where is my happy life that is rightfully mine now, thank you very much?!* They felt their country had, already, failed to live up to its billing. So yeah, they did what any dissatisfied person does: sue the government. That's right, instead of pursuing happiness, a slew of citizens pursued a lawsuit (!!!!). Classic America.

Unfortunately, leaving the interpretation of happiness so open-ended after pep-rallying everyone to go out and catch it led to a terrible amount of turbulence and an ineffable amount of distress, still very present in our lives today. As Darrin M. McMahon writes in *Happiness: A History*, "The meaning of their self-evident truth, ironically, has long been a matter of dispute. . . . Was [the pursuit of happiness] a meaningless phrase, a 'glittering generality' that has sent generations grasping after an illusion?"[2]

Happiness professor Ben Franklin explained to those displeased folks that yes, pursuing happiness is a right that the government intends to protect, but it wasn't just given out like free loaves of day-old bread. He told people to, you know, go out and "catch it yourself," like it's Wi-Fi you're mooching off your neighbor.

It's like he set up the kind of scavenger-hunt game I'd play with my eight-year-old niece. *OK, Nora, so Uncle Benny says our clues are (1) Happiness is as important as being alive and being free. (2) It's something we have to catch ourselves. (3) It's pursuable. Yes, honey, I know that sounds hard, but that's the point!* "There are no gains without pains," as Ben Franklin first wrote.

Ben was outspoken and opinionated about happiness's ties to success, which ties to being rich, which comes from reaching, in his words, "moral perfection."

So that we could be "morally perfect" à la Dr. Franklin, he

specified thirteen virtues that he would track daily, going as far as publishing samples of his daily diary for others to copy—OG bullet-journal style. "Diligence is the Mother of Good-luck," he wrote (long before having "lucky girl syndrome" would be promoted as a diligence-free way to success).[3]

Settled, it seemed, was not his forte. As Burns told journalist Arthur C. Brooks in *The Atlantic*, Franklin was the "least static of [the founding fathers], a moving object his entire life. . . . For Franklin, happiness meant lifelong learning. . . . In other words, self-improvement"[4]—to which he devoted a casual one or two hours each day, jam-packed with self-scrutiny and "air baths" (sitting naked in front of his open windows, the only one of his habits that we don't, to my knowledge, promote today).

But there's another big theme that Big Ben baked into the crust of our all-American apple pie: individualism and the idea that we can *create ourselves*.

Though hardly intended to contend with a Stephen King novel, a line in Walter Isaacson's book *Benjamin Franklin: An American Life* gives me recurring chills. After explaining Ben's approximately eight hundred earthly accomplishments—Franklin was a great scientist, inventor, diplomat, writer, and political thinker—Isaacson writes:

> He proved by flying a kite that lightning was electricity, and he invented a rod to tame it. He devised bifocal glasses and clean-burning stoves, charts of the Gulf Stream and theories about the contagious nature of the common cold. He launched various civic improvement schemes, such as a lending library, college, volunteer fire corps, insurance association, and matching grant fund-raiser. He helped invent America's unique style of home-spun humor and philosophical pragmatism. In foreign

policy, he created an approach that wove together ideal-
ism with balance-of-power realism. And in politics, he
proposed seminal plans for uniting the colonies and creating a federal model for a national government.[5]

"But the most interesting thing that Franklin invented and
continually reinvented," Isaacson says, "was himself."

In Ben, I see Matt Damon's creepy and alluring identity-
stealing character in *The Talented Mr. Ripley*. I see self-created
Jay Gatsby. (Sexy Leo's version.) I see Anna Sorokin (or Delvey?).
But I also see my neighbor Beth hawking essential oils on Facebook. And a friend of a friend snapping photos in a lobby of a
more lux hotel than the one she's actually staying in. I see myself, too. Dancing around on YouTube with a spatula three
minutes after sobbing on the floor.

For Ben, self-help may as well be called self-*making*—and
he inspires millions of ordinary people to work hard to *self-
make* themselves into a success. Ben was a prototype of faking
it to make it. His *Autobiography* might have been called the
original *Guide to Carefully Crafted Personal Creation for
Dummies*. He treated every day like it was New Year's Eve—
with an insatiable intensity for never-ending personal invention.

The spirit of self-creation was (and is) celebrated by new
Americans who were (and still are) all about letting freedom
reign. We fetishize free will. And what better way to use it than
to take complete responsibility for one's own reality!? For that,
Ben laid the cobblestones for what today we call individualism,
as in *Yeehaw! Our own success is up to us!* And also as in *Our
failure is because of us.*

I was raised in the era of "Be Yourself Because Everyone
Else Is Taken" bumper stickers. In my home, individualism was
highly praised. I was natured *and* nurtured to have confidence

in not being the norm. My mom was an only child raised by immigrant parents from Ukraine. She continuously felt like a misfit, whether she was among her expat Ukrainian community or her mainstream suburban one. So, to cope with her discomfort and loneliness, she turned the painful feeling of isolation into an empowered feeling of individualism and raised me on those same values.

It turns out that there's a drastic difference between being *an individual* and living in *an individualistic society*; that difference is *Every man is himself* versus *Every man for himself*—or *You're a unique snowflake, love yourself as you are* versus *Pull yourself up by your bootstraps! Be self-reliant! Take control of your fate!*

The former is a lovely and critical sentiment. Every man, woman, both, none of the above, or all of the above *is* their self and deserves autonomy, encouragement, and support for living self-loyally. The latter, however, is harmful because (a) it turns an individual's happiness into that individual's responsibility, and (b) it directly contradicts our fundamental human need for community.

Ben's continuous (read: obsessive) self-growth took priority over family and friends, making his pursuit of happiness the polar opposite of what researchers today have found, unquestionably, to be a top component of *actual* happiness: community. As a teen, he ran away from his family of origin, and as an adult, he didn't have a loving or respectful relationship with his wife and kids (read: abandonment, adultery, and absence). But he had successfully achieved such fame and admiration that over twenty thousand people attended his funeral. So, priorities.

I'm going on and on about Benny boy because it's thanks to him that we equate fulfillment with continual self-improvement and act like it's the structured, regimented, and consistent of the bunch who are the morally superior citizens. It's also because of Benny that we have the first rags-to-riches story and a self-made person as the mascot of the American dream, and that we lean toward putting more value into our finances than into our family. Ben rejected contentment back then, as do we right now.

But as Brooks writes in *The Atlantic*, "Whether he himself had achieved happiness is another matter." Unsurprisingly, though disappointingly, he kept his multitude of contradictions hidden from his public persona and absent from his *Autobiography*. "As with so many happiness professors and advice-givers," writes Brooks, "it is probably better to do what they say than to copy how they live."[6]

And that we do. Because while we may think all things Ben exist in the *history* section of a bookstore, his legacy also lives on in the self-improvement section. Nowadays, many books offer advice on achieving success and happiness and personal development—including rising early, monitoring our habits, acting confidently, and even eating vegetables! And guess who was the original writer of the maxim "Early to Bed, and early to rise, makes a Man healthy, wealthy and wise"?[7]

Ultimately, today, the self-improvement reels we see on our phones while we poop are updated versions of the old-fashioned ideas of one man (and a freak genius at that). Unbeknownst to most (?) of us, wherever we live, whatever gender we are, whatever our DNA, family dynamics, personalities, dreams, talents, quirks, and culture may be, Ben's idea of happiness has become the focus of our hopes.

The way I see it, Thomas Jefferson declared it, but Dr. Franklin put the pursuit of happiness in our tap water. And me, my Guide, my Guide's guides, *their* guides—generations of us who've been pursuing happiness by avoiding unhappiness—have been drinking it like Kool-Aid.

5

. . . .

If You're Eudaimonic and You Know It, Clap Your Hands

As you can see from the aforementioned history lesson, it makes sense why Western culture has a cultlike idolization of feeling happy. We've made it the number one goal of life. Happiness has gone so far past a desirable mood or the smile that comes from a fast-food meal with a free toy—happiness is our full-blown ideology. We've turned the human experience into a mission of avoiding pain and maximizing pleasure. Rather than treat happiness as pleasant vibes that result from doing things we enjoy or as one of the *many emotions we humans are capable of feeling*, we treat happiness as something specific that we can, in Ben's words, "catch."

Sure, objectively, *wanting* to feel happy is not an issue.

The issue is *trying* to feel happy.

And the distinction is robust.

Trying to be happy is a bad idea for two reasons:

1. It doesn't work.
2. When it doesn't work, we blame ourselves and then become even less happy *and, additionally,* ashamed. Because when we believe happiness results from our own effort, then a lack thereof is, of course, our own failure.

There are two main nonworking ways we pursue happiness:

1. With thoughts
2. With things

PURSUING HAPPINESS WITH THOUGHTS

When I really understood Ben Franklin's influence on our pursuit of happiness, I found myself in a much better headspace. I thought, *This could be why I've been doing happiness all wrong: because I've been taking opinion-based advice from an old genius's writings that've been going around like a game of telephone. Like, I've basically been following a folktale.*

So, I considered, why not lean on the docs? How about I go to the people who have probably been hiding in plain sight all along, waiting to inform me of my depression when I was just willing to ask. *Like, OK, guys, I've been rubbing a $48 jade stone on my forehead for months now. I think I'm just going to get the Botox.*

Then I enrolled in grad school because I thought maybe my problem was I'd been following hearsay happiness advice from self-appointed self-help gurus and if I went to an objective field, the science world, I could learn the real stuff, the researched stuff. That sexy empirical data.

I thought maybe the scientists could tell me why it seemed like the days I was too exhausted to focus on my positive thinking were the days I went to bed more untroubled than the days that I made positive thinking my priority. Was there some backward brain thing they could explain to me? Like, *Hey, little-known fact: our amygdalae are stuck in opposite-day mode. That's why it seems the harder you try to be happier, the more unhappy you become!*

Or I don't know, I guess I hoped they could tell me, scientifically, the best-proven way to word an affirmation so that it actually worked. Or if, for reals, mind and body habits can overpower antidepressant medications?

This is why, when I arrived with my Calpak laptop backpack and Hydro Flask at age thirty-one at Teachers College at Columbia University for my graduate-level positive psychology class, I was buzzing.

To start, we all went around the class and explained why we were there. It was surprising to me that a lot of my peers had only vaguely heard of positive psychology and were mildly curious to know more. Others had taken a previous class with the professor and liked him as a person, so were following him into this next topic of study. When the stage was mine, I hard-core fangirled the subject matter, explaining that I was there to *actually,* for real *for real,* learn how to improve one's happiness.

Defined as "the scientific study of what makes life worth living" by its founder Martin Seligman, positive psychology, I understood, aims to increase human flourishing, which makes it different from traditional (negative?) psychology, whose goal is to reduce human suffering.

So while traditional psychology delves into past negative experiences and emotions, positive psychology emphasizes building on positive experiences and strengths to achieve personal growth and happiness. As Seligman wrote in his book *Authentic Happiness*, "You probably ponder . . . how to go from plus two to plus seven in your life, not just how to go from minus five to minus three."[1]

Though such complex arithmetic makes me dizzy, I believe Seligman's point is, basically, *who would want to just be a little less negative? Why settle at good when you can be great!?* (A sentiment he probably picked up from sipping Ben Franklin's spiked tap water in the fountains at the University of Pennsylvania, the university Franklin founded, where, incredibly, positive psychology was also established. Synchronicity!)

After introductions, our first lecture began. I had my pen in hand and my pad on my desk, ready to scribble down the scientific tricks to a life well lived.

One by one, the professor dropped what I can only best describe as tweetables.

Quoting Mihaly Csikszentmihalyi, the psychologist behind the concept of flow, "Treatment is not just fixing what is broken; it is nurturing what is best."

Preach.

Then a Camus line got dropped, arousing me in a borderline inappropriate way.

Camus? What are you doing in positive psychology?

"Camus wrote that the foremost question of philosophy is why one should not commit suicide. One cannot answer that question just by curing depression; there must be positive reasons for living as well." My professor explained that *positive psychology* is an umbrella term for theories and research about what makes life most worth living.

Yes! Gimme all the theories and research. I. Am. Here. For. It.

Thankfully, to quench my thirst for Real Information, I was given some percentages and numbers.

It was explained that about 10 percent of our well-being is genetics, about 10 percent is stuff we have (material items), about 30 percent is external circumstances, and about 50 percent is our thoughts and actions. This is why, I learned, a main concept in positive psychology is shifting our perception. Then the class concluded with a quote on its own final PowerPoint slide: "If you change the way you look at things, the things you look at change." A classic line from mega-bestselling self-help author Wayne Dyer, whose endorsement blurb adorned the cover of my Guide's books.

A eerie chill washed over me. How had self-help followed me here?!

By the end of class, I could have put my notes side by side with my most underlined quotes from my self-help books' stash and it would have been the same concepts, just now being taught by people in lab coats instead of kimonos.

That first night after class, my mind was racing. *Is positive psychology the scientific study of existentialism?! Or is it an empirical argument for toxic positivity?!*

And then I woke up the next morning, peed on a stick, and learned I was pregnant.

I can't say for sure whether it was the exhaustion of growing my baby from a lentil to a lemon, or if it was the letdown from having way too high expectations for positive psychology, but as the semester went on, I could barely make it through each lecture.

The supersecret scientific hacks for happiness appeared to be more like a supershock that people with PhDs got paid money to prove common sense. For example, there was the

"Counting Blessings" exercise, in which subjects kept a daily gratitude journal and wrote three things for which they were grateful each day. In one study, participants who completed this exercise reported increased levels of happiness and decreased symptoms of depression.

I was concerned about the overlap with the damaging parts of self-help I was seeing, particularly positive psychology's aversion to negative emotions and the overemphasis on positivity. Which, like, *really, Talia? Is the chocolate fudge ice cream too chocolaty for you, too?*

The powerful push of *happiness is a choice-ing* was deeply triggering. I was told that 80 percent of people with depression relapse with medication and therapy, so the need to take control of one's own happiness was dire.

We talked about how negative thoughts are stronger than positive thoughts, comparing them to pebbles and feathers, respectively. Obviously, to tip the scale in the feathers' favor would require a heck of a lot more feathers than pebbles. But rather than go to a Michaels art and crafts supply store and buy a boa, I was told I needed to work my tush off to get those pebbles off the scale. All this did was put a heavy pit in my stomach.

It turns out that this is a common criticism of positive psychology.

In *America the Anxious*, Ruth Whippman writes, "In many ways, the field [of positive psychology] has become self-help's more respectable cousin. . . . The books sit on the same shelf of the bookstore as their less august predecessors and are often virtually indistinguishable in tone and substance."[2]

Listen, I can't fault anyone for thinking that if you want to feel happier feelings, you should think happier thoughts. What could be more logical than telling your friend to cheer up when they say they're sad? Or trying to nudge yourself to focus on the good when you feel the opposite.

Unfortunately, hearing "just cheer up" isn't always the best way to cheer up.

When positivity turns toxic

Toxic positivity wants us to stifle negative thoughts like a fart. If you're not positive, you're not trying hard enough. Optimism overload tells us that anything other than happy emotions are an error, and if we just try a little harder, we can eliminate them completely.

Toxic refers to the harm that positivity pressure can cause by discouraging people from processing negative emotions and experiences healthily, and the danger that can arise from dismissing or invalidating authentic emotions and experiences. "Denial is the most destructive form of self-harm," says Alice Feeney's Aimee Sinclair character in *I Know Who You Are*.

A much-imposed strategy in our pursuit of happiness is the diminishment of negativity. I suppose the logic of this is fair enough. If you want to win more basketball games, then you should miss fewer shots. However, in keeping with this analogy, society pressures us to swap the intense players with upbeat, smiley, positive cheerleaders. But plastered smiles and shiny pom-poms don't keep basketballs from hitting rims or smacking backboards. No more than gratitude keeps sad stuff from making you sad.

The emotional stress that comes from cutting negative emotions out of our life like gluten, particularly when negative emotions are natural, appropriate, and completely fair, has been linked not only to major mental illnesses but also to chronic-stress-related physical problems like heart disease, digestive issues, headaches, insomnia, and autoimmune disorders, all of which are on the rise.

Because, basically, you're constipating your tears. And constipation of any kind is never the road to wellness.

Reading "Look on the bright side!" in a self-help book is like a car manual telling you to look at your empty gas tank as half full. Or better yet, it's like the AAA tow truck driver telling you to ignore your flat tire and just be grateful because at least you have three other full ones. In fact, it'd be like AAA Joe saying, "Write down three reasons you're more grateful for your car than you are upset about the flat tire, and then you'll be so overcome with gratitude you won't even care about being stuck on the side of the road!"

Oh. You can't come up with three reasons that flattened your frustration with your flat tire? Well, that's your fault. (Funny how self-encouragement quickly flips from a supportive "you have so much to be grateful for!" to a "you're not positive enough!!!" victim—yes, even of flat tires—blaming.) "With great power comes great responsibility," Uncle Ben tells Peter Parker. He may have been covertly motivating the young Spider-Man in training, but he was also giving words to us common folk, who have the great power of self-regulation, which also seems to come with the great responsibility to regulate ourselves as upbeat!

Because what happens when we fail at our responsibility (i.e., acknowledge often shitty reality as it is) is that we blame ourselves. We've got the power, right? (Callback to the law of attraction from chapter 3.)

I've read this described as the "tyranny of the positive," which is a fancier "fake it till you make it." It's like being pressured to smile through a root canal—to stay upbeat even in the face of difficult or negative situations.

As Svend Brinkmann writes in his book *Stand Firm: Resisting the Self-Improvement Craze*, "It is a kind of universally accepted international pocket psychology in most Western countries that we should all 'think positively,' be 'resource-oriented' and see problems as interesting 'challenges.'"[3]

We're sold that positive thinking works in all areas of our lives—from our finances to our health, relationships, careers, and even the lifespan of our snake plants. We've become so proficient in finding silver linings, in turning our pain into purpose—I mean, profit—that even negative posts on Instagram are spun positively. A friend who was a semi-famous daredevil performer got tragically injured practicing a stunt for an episode of *America's Got Talent*, and his first post from the hospital in full bandages and cast was a thumbs-up. His second post was him immediately rebranded from being an inspirational strongman to a self-proclaimed "roll" (as in wheelchair) model.

There's a scene in the movie *The Break-Up* where Jennifer Aniston (Brooke) and Vince Vaughn (Gary) host a passive-aggressive dinner party at their very airy and aspirational Chicago apartment. After their guests leave, their kitchen is "messy" in the way that Jennifer Aniston ever has a "bad hair day." Brooke heads to the sink to wash the dishes while Gary heads to the couch to play a video game. This conversation happens:

BROOKE
I busted my ass all day cleaning this house and then cooking that meal, and I worked today. It'd be nice if you said "thank you." And helped me with the dishes.

GARY

Fine. I'll help you do the damn dishes.

BROOKE

Oh, come on. You know what? No, see? That's the . . .
that's not what I want.

GARY

You just said that you want me to help you do the dishes.

BROOKE

I want you to want to do the dishes.

I want *you* to *want* to think positively. Not to be coerced,
guilted, shamed, pressured, tricked, bribed, conned, or pushed
into it. I want you to want to express gratitude, not write three
things down because you bought a $19 journal from some
guide promising that if you do, you'll be happy.

Gratitude is a form of focused appreciation for the good in
our lives. It's a common thread between Jewish, Christian,
Muslim, Buddhist, Hindu, and Oprah belief systems. It's the
subject of well over 270 scientific research studies and countless
well-meaning memes and mugs.

I look at gratitude like food fat, of which there are two
types: good fats and bad fats.

Gratitude is good if it's used to genuinely count your blessings. If it bubbles up when you look around and feel apprecia-
tive of some of your life's simple things: your dog, the sunshine,
picking the faster-moving lane in the traffic jam, things that
might not get your recognition that often. This is the "Thank

you, socks" kind of gratitude that we Marie Kondo advocates whisper as we fold a pair of cotton no-shows. Which is really more of a *Thank you for not eating one of them, washing machine.*

This gratitude is good for us. Clinical trials have shown that practicing it can have dramatic and lasting positive effects on a person's well-being, both physically and mentally (mainly because of its impact on our stress levels). In some studies, genuine gratitude has been shown to enhance one's mental health, lower blood pressure, improve immune function, promote feelings of happiness and well-being, and ignite acts of helpfulness, generosity, and cooperation. It's also said to help reduce the lifetime risk for depression, anxiety, and substance abuse disorders.

Then there's harmful gratitude that, like unhealthy sugar, hides under a slew of different names, though its main moniker is toxic positivity. This is forced appreciation, and it does not make us well. It can contribute to increased shame, loneliness, depression, anxiety, cardiovascular disease, inflammation, and other forms of poor mental and physical health.

There are many peas in the pod of harmful gratitude, but I think one of the worst is comparative suffering, sometimes referred to as "first-world problems," or as my dad calls them, "high-quality issues." Comparative suffering is when we line our struggles up to someone else's in order to determine who deserves empathy. It's when you don't allow yourself to truly feel your hurts because you know other people have it worse, so who are you to complain? It's when you try to bury your own pain under a pile of gratitude, convince yourself that your feelings are invalid, or, worse, straight up shout at your selfish, ungrateful self to *snap out of it.*

This was my area of expertise. I had Olympic-level talent for berating myself for feeling sad when I knew that others would kill to have my life.

But trying to look on the sunny side when you're really on the shady side not only doesn't work but actively causes us harm. I read about a study in Susan David's book *Emotional Agility* that delights me. Some researchers examined two years' worth of yearbook photos from a private women's college to point out genuine smiles from forced ones. Incredibly, it's possible to detect the difference. (Do try this at home!) When we give an authentic, teeth-showing, ear-to-ear, crow's-feet "CHEESE," it activates two different eye muscles. But one of those muscles (the orbicularis oculi, duh) can't be manipulated voluntarily—it can't be forced! So if that tiny muscle near the ladies' eyes wasn't activated, the researchers knew the grin was bullshit.

(Thankfully, this investigation was conducted using photos in the 1958–1960 yearbooks because, with today's normalization of forehead-muscle relaxers, I'm sure it's become impossible to discern real from fake from frozen.)[4]

When the researchers caught up with these students thirty years later, they found that the authentic smilers had better lives regarding their marriages, general happiness, and careers. You can't fake it till you make your way out of negative emotions—it won't help.

Thought suppression

OK, so if spamming ourselves with positive thoughts isn't the key, then perhaps squashing our negative thoughts is the way to go? Because as much as we're encouraged to think positively, we're also discouraged from thinking negatively. Gurus and motivational speakers remind us that our negative thinking is what got us in the shitter we find ourselves in today that has led us to their positive-thinking solution. But unfortunately, this is also an ineffective way to feel happier. Because here's the zinger: the happier we try to be, the unhappier we usually become. Pursuing happiness backfires.

Russian novelist Fyodor Dostoevsky, with whom you might be familiar from reading the SparkNotes of his thick book *Crime and Punishment* for your high school English class, has an enlightening quote from his book *Winter Notes on Summer Impressions*. He wrote: "Try to pose for yourself this task: not to think of a polar bear, and you will see that the cursed thing will come to mind every minute."[5]

His point, if you ask me, is more poignant than anything that emerged from the over two hundred thousand words in *Crime and Punishment*. It's actually been turned into a psychological phenomenon called the ironic process theory.

The ironic process theory says that when you try to suppress certain thoughts, behaviors, or desires, they (ironically) become more dominant. So it could also be called the theory of the cranky, overtired children who can't help doing the opposite of what you ask them to. (Or of the fully rested adult like myself who tells herself, "NO ICE CREAM THIS WEEK SO YOU CAN CONFIDENTLY WEAR A BATHING SUIT NEXT WEEK," and then leaves her house in slippers at 2:00 a.m. to hit the twenty-four-hour grocery store for a pint of oat-milk mint chocolate chip.)

If you try not to think about a white bear, you can't help thinking about a white bear.

If you try to eliminate negative thoughts, you will have more negative thoughts.

If you try to force out a sneeze when you feel the tickle, the sneeze (amazingly) won't come!

(Trust me! Life hack: this is how I trick myself out of sneezing at inopportune moments, which is all moments.)

Dostoevsky's witty thought experiment isn't the only basis for this paradox. A professor of psychology at Harvard researched thought suppression in 1987 and homed in on this counterintuitive conduct of our minds. In his book *White Bears and Other Unwanted Thoughts*, Daniel Wegner explains that this behavior isn't our minds being rebellious assholes, but rather a malfunctioning of our metacognition (when we think about thinking).

Wegner found that when we purposefully try to block a thought, one part of our mind avoids that suppressed thought, but another part "checks in" occasionally to make sure that the shunned thought is still being suppressed. This check-in is what, ironically, brings that exact thought to mind.[6]

I'll pause here for a laugh break because we humans are ridiculous.

Of course, this ironic process doesn't just happen when we tell ourselves to relax, be happier, not cry, stop laughing, hold still, or focus. It's arguably strongest when I tell myself I am not, under any circumstances, going to bring up the surprise stripper Jesse told me appeared at a bachelor party on a double date, and then before we even get our apps, I have brought up the surprise stripper Jesse told me appeared at a bachelor party.

"When we admonish ourselves not to do something, not to believe something, not to feel something, even not to think something," Wegner writes, "our attempt to say no is often no more effective than a flyswatter held up to stop a cannonball."

I think back to all the times I tried repeatedly to tell myself to stop having certain thoughts and feelings, only to exacerbate those exact thoughts and feelings (and then spew fury at myself for self-sabotaging). In this sense, putting the kibosh on our feelings is not only less effective than fly-swatting a cannonball, but it's also more harmful than sipping sanitizer to fight germs.

FINLAND IS HOME to some of the happiest people on earth. In 2023, for the sixth time, it was crowned the "happiest country in the world"—a title that speaks volumes about Finland's joyous spirit and the contentment of its people.

They're the happiest even though at times during the year it's dark almost the entire day. While we here in the United States are encouraged to, during the darker winter months, sit under $49 indoor sun lamps to cheer up, the Finns have a more effective method of dealing with the darkness: heavy metal music.

It dominates the mainstream radio stations, heavy metal bands steadily sell out shows, and it is even a main genre at local karaoke bars, making Finland the heavy metal capital of the world. At the 2016 Nordic Summit, President Barack Obama noted this silly correlation: "I do want to point out, that Finland has perhaps the most heavy metal bands in the world, per capita," he said, "and also ranks high on good governance. I don't know if there's a correlation there."[7]

Ida-Katharina Kiljander, a music teacher and the lead vocalist of Finnish metal band Mournful Lines, hypothesized, "The reason why heavy metal might reflect the Finnish mentality is probably because we are so private that it is difficult to discuss our feelings, but still we need an outlet to deal with these negative emotions."[8] In that sense, maybe we could all use a little heavy metal in our life. I once had a friend confess to me her jealousy of babies because they get to cry at feelings that grown-ups must suppress.

That's a rosé-induced way of saying what psychologist

Barbara Held wrote about in her book *Stop Smiling, Start Kvetching*, that life being hard is not the problem. The problem is that we're pressured to act as if life isn't hard.[9] *Kvetching*, like *schlep*, is one of Yiddish's legendary onomatopoeias, up there with *chutzpah*, *klutz*, *schlub*, *schmooze*, *schmuck*, and *tush*. To *kvetch* means to complain or bitch (the verb).

"Painting over the cracks doesn't mean they're not there," Alice Feeney writes in *I Know Who You Are*, "even though life is prettier when you do."[10]

Tell that to social media therapists and podcasters who advise us to snip-snip toxic people right out of our lives like a deviated septum. And then be grateful. Dream big. And fake-laugh with your mouth open.

When pursuing happiness doesn't work

The harder I tried to be happy, the more miserable I felt. I felt like I was slipping into unhappiness quicksand. I cried when my headphone batteries died on a run; I cried when our dog got a haircut; and I cried when I saw my cheerful face on my cookbook cover—so then I ran around my home, turning all my copies face down. I cried when I missed a section when applying sunscreen to Jesse's back and that gave him a bright red zebra stripe. I cried when I thought about all the texts I'd read and not yet replied to that now were lost because we couldn't yet mark texts as unread. (I cried about that, too.) On more than one occasion, I cried because putting on blush was too hard because I couldn't even simulate enough of a smile to find my cheekbones.

One day at a long-overdue physical, I let it slip to the nurse practitioner that my husband thought I was maybe struggling and could use a smidgle of something to take the edge off.

I couldn't see her facial expression with my legs spread in the way, but I did hear her voice become extra kind as she said, "Oh, so are you struggling with anxiety or depression?"

"Ummm . . ." I paused, trying to come up with a medical way to say, *Gratitude's not working.*

"Anxiety," I replied.

She started rattling off all the symptoms of anxiety.

Do you feel nervous, restless, or tense?

No.

Have a sense of impending danger, panic, or doom?

No.

Have an increased heart rate and breathing?

No.

Sweating? Trembling? Feeling weak or tired? Trouble concentrating or thinking about anything other than the present worry? Trouble sleeping? Difficulty controlling worry? Having the urge to avoid things that trigger anxiety?

No, no, no.

Glee washed over me. I had none! Zilch symptoms of anxiety. All the self-improvement I'd worked like a full-time job for the past ten years paid off! I was so overjoyed that I hardly heard the nurse ask, "What about depression?"

I thought, *You mean the "I'm too lazy to choose happiness" cop-out?*

"There's no way I'm depressed," I said with a chuckle, considering whether I should whip out my phone and take her on a tour of my cheerful Instagram feed.

Do you have feelings of sadness, tearfulness, emptiness, or hopelessness? I heard her ask.

Umm.

Loss of interest or pleasure in most or all normal activities?

Uh-huh.

Sleep disturbances, including insomnia or sleeping too much?

Yes.

Tiredness and lack of energy, so even minor tasks take major effort?

Very much, I said, remembering my recent failed blush incident.

Reduced appetite? Trouble concentrating, remembering details, and making decisions? Unexplained physical problems, such as back pain or headaches? Feelings of worthlessness or guilt, fixating on past failures or self-blame?

Yes, yes, yes.

Frequent or recurrent thoughts of death or suicidal ideation?

I paused.

"I mean, I don't have suicidal *thoughts*," I said nonchalantly. "But yeah, I often wish I could die. Like, not really *die* die, but disappear for periods of time," I continued, like I'm explaining how I curl my hair. "Like, just stop being here, alive, abstractly. But I never envision *killing* myself, you know?"

Her entire face sank. So did my stomach.

"Doesn't everyone think about dying sometimes?" I asked with genuine bafflement. Although the answer had, at this point, become blatantly obvious.

I felt terrified, relieved, and like I wanted to vomit all at once. For my entire life, since I could formulate human thoughts, I'd sometimes hated myself so much I wanted to evaporate. And sometimes fighting not to feel that way would get too exhausting, so I'd wish for a trapdoor in the floor to fall into. Sometimes the pain of being a human became so unbearable, I just wanted to put on noise-canceling headphones—but for all of my horrible swirly thoughts. Oftentimes, I was so overcome with apathy that moving from the bed to the shower felt impossible. I had to put a folding plastic chair in there when standing felt too exhausting.

Never once did I wonder if this was Normal°.

My high school superlative was "most likely to brighten your day." I was consistently "a pleasure to have in class." Any sadness I had was circumstantial. Like, I was sad because I didn't get a cool work opportunity. Or because I had an overwhelming amount of emails. The weather brought me down. As did returning from a trip. Losing followers hurt. All these things I could "choose" my way out of, though, with enough journaling, mantras, meditations, and prayers.

I never thought I could be, like, A Depressed Person.

The nurse put her hand on my shoulder as she said, "Life doesn't have to be so hard for you."

I did all I could to not fold up like a Slinky.

Trembling, I made my way out to the corner of Broadway and Sixtieth Street. It was a swelteringly hot, early August day. I felt like I was in one of those movie scenes where the character is tripping on shrooms and the background blurs and spins and closes in on them. So basically how I'd heard tripping on shrooms described.

Life doesn't have to be so hard. The nurse's words played on repeat, like when I hear Seal's "Kiss from a Rose" and then have it stuck in my head for nine days.

I moved my mouth around a word that suddenly felt so new. *Depression. Depression. Depression.* Kind of ironic that a word that essentially translates to an absence of happiness gave me an instant abundance of it.

There are at least a few experiences in our lives that have clearly defined before-and-afters: the loss of a loved one, the birth of a new one, life after learning you can just eat peanut butter off a spoon, your face before you realized the foundation you'd been wearing for the last six months was two shades too orange. I'll add to that list realizing that you're not broken for the first time in your life.

So I was standing there tripping on emotional shrooms when I suddenly thought, *The closest thing to this moment must be finding out that you were adopted.* Reality shatters: Who's Mom? Who's Dad? Questions arise: Am I really lactose intolerant? I *knew* swimming wasn't "in my DNA"! Conspiracies are considered: What's the truth? Who can I trust?

But why was I so shook? I strained to understand. It's not like if I thought I had strep and I went to a doc and it turned out I had laryngitis I would feel like the rug had been pulled out from under me.

I was trembling because I realized I wasn't broken. I was trying to process the realization that my lack of general jubilation wasn't a lack of self-will. It was, as I'd later understand, a perfect storm of my biology, psychology, and personal life experience. It was a bunch of things tripping the wire that my genes were preloaded with.

Shock turned to anger. Rage. Fury. All this time these experts I trusted were teaching me to take responsibility, which meant to assume the blame when it was *never* MY FAULT. My inability to think my way into inner peace wasn't because of an improper thinking technique. I wasn't just shitty at blocking my negative thoughts. An apple a day couldn't keep my suicidal ideation away. It wasn't more lavender essential oil I needed—it was Lexapro!

Then I felt betrayed. Wildly and entirely betrayed. I had thought these self-help gurus genuinely cared for me. I had trusted the methods they preached, the ones they said cured them of their ails and gave them a life beyond their wildest dreams.

Next, I felt lost. I unsubscribed, unfollowed, and tossed all my self-improvement books into boxes. The scene was reminiscent of an alcoholic ceremoniously pouring their last bottle of vodka down the sink, letting their past pain wash away with every glug. As I handled each book, I felt the eerie void of its once almighty magical power. No longer were these texts talismans of hope; they now embodied harm, and all hope currently came from reclaiming my power over them. I asked Alexa to play "Amazing Grace," and for about seven times hearing it on repeat, I bawled out a decade of pain for mistaking depression the disease for depression the character weakness.

The catharsis of self-forgiveness was overwhelming. Once I apologized to myself for over fifteen years of blaming myself, I celebrated how this new self-understanding just saved me another fifteen years, thirty years, or, God willing, sixty-five years of beating myself up or blaming myself.

Getting my diagnosis ignited an avalanche of self-love and self-compassion that I didn't even know was possible. Finally, for once, I felt gratitude. And I didn't even need to force myself to journal about it!

The pain of self-blame

It's really fucking simple: when you are beat over the head with the idea that happiness is in your control, and you cannot feel happy no matter how hard you try, you blame yourself.

Just as with the New Thought movement, when spirit healer Quimby convinced everyone to suppress their negative thoughts lest they manifest negative things . . .

I'd spent the bulk of my life trapped in thoughts of despair, pain, and hopelessness, and I was desperate to get out. And since I hardly had the energy to change or do anything, being told that doing the one thing I was already comfortable with (*thinking*) could flip-flop my problem seemed, well, legitimate— with a side of Hail Mary.

It certainly didn't seem improbable that the order of appearance could be thought, *then* reality, since all my thoughts *and* my reality were sad.

And it absolutely didn't seem toxic or dangerous to whisper sweet nothings to myself in my own head.

But that's what it is. Assuming responsibility for reality can ruin you when you blame yourself for not being able to lucky-girl your way out of rain on your wedding day, the awful actions of others, or a mental illness.

But the problem is that claiming victory for reality feels great when you attribute serendipity to your thoughts!

And it's the promise of that rush, that high you feel that keeps you wondering, *If I just tried a little longer—or tweaked my mantra a smidge or changed my desire*, etc. That's what keeps you trapped in the serendipity/synchronicity spiral!

Do I think if I'd gone in another direction I wouldn't have wound up with a shocking diagnosis? I can't be sure. Research and science show that undoubtedly mental illness is a combo platter of genes and genetic and environmental triggers. Biopsychosocial model. But I am positive that had I been taught from an early age that happiness wasn't the norm of life but that angst was, and if I weren't pushed to pursue all things happiness from the earliest age, being depressed would be more like, as Freud wished, "the common cold." Had happiness been more normalized, I wouldn't have read manuals on how to achieve it and then felt awful when I couldn't, because it's impossible. That gap wouldn't have made me feel like a failure, which is a trigger for the genetics my insides were already in possession of. It's almost like you could say the impossible pursuit of happiness triggers depression.

PURSUING HAPPINESS WITH THINGS

In the faraway past, people believed happiness was dictated by fate and provided to them by the gods. The root *hap* in the word *happiness* originally signified luck, as in *happen*stance— as in, *Whoa, finding that penny just randomly happened!* (Also in the faraway past, pennies used to be exciting.) But originally, the idea of *trying to* become happier on your own was not a thing. Good shit was hopefully something that *happened to you.*

Over time, as many philosophers philosophized about this, happiness evolved into a thing that we could take control of ourselves using a variety of methods, from reasoning (Socrates) to accepting suffering (Buddha) to making funny Adam Sandler movies (Jews).

While we long ago ditched the "just lounge around in togas eating grapes and waiting for a god to happen to give us happiness" lifestyle (which is a bummer), we still haven't hitched ourselves to an agreed-upon definition of the damn thing.

One of the first songs most of us bop to as babies is "If You're Happy and You Know It, Clap Your Hands, Stomp Your Feet, Post to Instagram!" Being "happy" is delivered as common sense, part of being human. It's introduced to us before our ABCs because it's assumed to be something we don't need to be taught—the sides of our mouths automatically rise up with pleasurable feelings.

I wish we could say that happiness is like beauty: in the eye of the beholder. Or that happiness is like good sex: you can't describe it, but you know it when you feel it. Instead, we often say something like "Happiness is . . . the state of being happy? . . . The opposite of depression?"

Few words have less clarity than *happiness*. It's a bafflingly broad term that gets applied to a laughable array of feelings and experiences. As Tim Lomas, the author of *Happiness— Found in Translation: A Glossary of Joy from Around the World*, writes, "Sometimes a broad label is useful. A person can like reggae, ska, jazz, blues, swing, funk, punk, rock, and soul, but it can be handy to simply state that they're really into 'music.' Likewise, sometimes it can be sufficient and reassuring to just say, 'I'm happy.'"[11]

Yes, a general "I'm happy" is sufficient if you're journaling in a bubble bath or talking with your mom on the phone while waiting at the dog groomer. But when we're expected to orient our entire lives around pursuing this thing, a lack of clarity is extraordinarily problematic.

In his book, Lomas divides the complex landscape of happiness into three regions: happiness as a feeling; happiness as an inner warmth from our relationships (which are regularly touted as our principal source of happiness); and meaningful happiness, which stems from the satisfaction of living virtuously and authentically.

The root of the fundamental distinction lies in two opposing ancient Greek philosophical terms for happiness: *hedonia* and *eudaimonia*, which are unfortunately not a potato, potahto situation. Hedonia is all about acquiring a feeling. It's *feeling good*. It's basking in a state of delight and measuring happiness by comparing one's ratio of positive to negative emotions. This informs more of our general present-day understanding of happiness—experiencing pleasure.

Hedonia is the endorphin rush from a raise at work, a hit of dopamine from new shoes, or a gust of flattery from getting invited to a party. Hedonic happiness can be found in the good vibes that blow through our soul (and hair) as we ride in a convertible or when strangers double-tap the discreetly staged photo of our cute puppy.

Then there's eudaimonia, which was Aristotle's jam. Eudaimonia technically means "human flourishing" or well-being. Unlike hedonia, which is a feeling, eudaimonia is an action: living as an authentic expression of oneself. "Leading an *eudaimonic* life, Aristotle argued, requires cultivating the best qualities within you both morally and intellectually and living up to your potential," Emily Esfahani Smith writes in *The Power of Meaning: Crafting a Life That Matters*.

It's a fulfillment flavor of happiness—a more visceral and deep sense of a life well lived. Eudaimonia is that no-regrets-on-your-deathbed satisfaction. It's taking your last breaths without feeling the ache that palliative nurse Bronnie Ware found to be disturbingly common for those at their very end.

"I wish I'd had the courage to live a life true to myself, not the life others expected of me," Ware writes in her book *The Top Five Regrets of the Dying: A Life Transformed by the Dearly Departing*.[12] "This was the most common regret of all. When people realize that their life is over and look back clearly on it, it is easy to see how many dreams go unfulfilled." She explains that so many people hadn't honored even half of their dreams and had to die understanding that was due to choices they had made or not made.

That ownership/awareness of the consequence of their own choices is textbook existentialish . . . **RESPONSIBILITY!!!**

Existentialists love eudaimonia. Albert Camus defines happiness as "the simple harmony between a [person] and the life

[they] lead."[13] Simone de Beauvoir says it's the flourishing that comes from living in harmony with the world. According to Beauvoir, harmony means owning our freedom, being responsible for our lives, seeking out the truth, and having genuine connections with the world and others.[14]

Notice that missing from that brief list there is a *thing*. With bar codes, flash sales, and colors to choose from. *Material things*.

Following the hedonia flavor of happiness feeds right into one of the biggest myths about it: that more stuff will make us more happy—often by making us less aware of our lack of eudaimonic happiness. We give our moolah to companies that profit off our desire for diversion. Because if we spend our weekends cleaning out our pantries or organizing our garages, we won't have time or energy for feeling the existential angst that comes from a lack of meaning and fulfillment in our lives.

So much of life is **distracting** us from the underlying existential angst and responsibility we know is on **us**.

I think of this thing-to-happiness equation as "byproducting." Byproducting blurs the lines so that something either directly ups our happiness (as in, *If you have money, then you'll be happy*) or uses a middleman (as in, *If you use our sunscreen, you won't get wrinkles, so you won't look old, and that will make you happy!*).

Our widespread belief is that happiness results from achieving this, looking like that, possessing this, and never having to do that. Sponsored and unsponsored content is full of smiling influencers promoting happiness via some sort of packaged good. This is the hardest part of trying to escape pedestaling happiness—being inundated with messages that remind us that (a) we're supposed to be happy, and (b) we are currently not.

That's actually one of the most ironic backward results of

pursuing happiness in general: that it highlights our lack thereof!

Of course, on some level, we know this stuff doesn't bring happiness. We read "Happiness Comes from Within" maxims on doctors' office posters, and we get it taught to us in Disney movies. Sebastian from *The Little Mermaid* suggests that the seaweed always appears more appealing in someone else's body of water. But seaweed, success, money, a house, a car, a flawless complexion, a jet-setting lifestyle, power, fame, popularity, an organized junk drawer—anything and everything gets pitched as a viable path to happiness. And it's not *knowledge* that stops us from pursuing happiness à la material by-products; it's keeping that knowledge in the forefront of our minds every day— and maybe taking Amazon off your phone.

All sorts of psychological theories can explain why our expectations let us down. One is called hedonic adaptation: that we get used to pleasure—meaning we don't experience lasting satisfaction from a thing. Despite acquiring things that should make them happy, people tend to stay at the same level of happiness.

Constantly trying to find pleasure can be a never-ending cycle, 'cause, unfortunately, our enjoyment doesn't last. Psychologists have a phrase for it: "the hedonic treadmill," meaning that we can make progress, but it never really makes us feel any different—like how we can sprint on the conveyor belt at 8.3 and still be stuck behind a girl with see-through leggings watching *The Price Is Right* with no sound.

"Great gifts and achievements early in life are simply not an insurance policy against suffering later on," Arthur C. Brooks writes in *From Strength to Strength*. "The fact that we can't store up our glories and enjoy them when they are long past gets to the problem of dissatisfaction."[15]

Money is also not an insurance policy against suffering. Studies keep proving that people with the most money aren't the most happy. We're led to believe with great money comes great opportunity, so we expect happiness to come from larger salaries or sales on eBay. So the more money we have, the more expectations of happiness we have, and the greater that discrepancy is, the more we despair. We expect to be living the high life every day, and so when we're not (because of human-condition stuff), we feel distraught. This gappy makes us ultra unhappy.

It's pursuing the hedonic kind of happiness—the pleasurable sugar rushes—that doesn't stick. Eudaimonia, the purpose-sparked happiness—or the fiber, if you will—lasts.

But we need both. A balance of enjoyment and meaning. Both sugar and fiber. Like a raspberry.

I feel confident that we have a solid handle on the hedonic-achievement part of this equation. It's the eudaimonia that needs some work. Because ultimately, good vibes alone aren't enough to help us quell our existential angst. Rather, it's the search for eudaimonia, the *meaning* happiness, that will bring us the joy we expect.

The thing is, it's not so simple to put your finger on eudaimonia. Eudaimonia is more of a deep visceral state of joy and fullness. Eudaimonia is about your spirit thriving! Good luck putting that on a drive-through menu paired with a plastic toy for $3.65.

At least with *happiness*, we can conjure up some definition (usually of the hedonic kind) to know when we've got "it." We easily attribute happy to being in a great mood, having a blast, feeling cheerful, and, yay, smiling! Happiness is relatively easy to detect because it's a feeling and an emotion, and we have quick, easy access through cake and sex and typing in a promo code to save 20 percent.

In contrast, I believe one of the colossal problems with getting enthused about building a eudaimonic-focused life is that we don't know how to know when we have it.

Have it?

Feel it?

Reach it?

Bop it? Pull it? Twist it?

There's no "If You're Thriving and You Know It" song to educate our littles, nor is there a designated facial expression that we can teach them to communicate meaning nonverbally. (Like a smile.) Smiling is a learned behavior that grows alongside our social and emotional development—like mastering the "I farted, but I'm staying inconspicuous" poker face, or the "Pretty please let me finish this movie past my bedtime" puppy eyes.

Smiling is actually not one of the innate reflexes babies are born with, like sucking and grasping and exploding poop out of diapers and up backs. Of course, newborns come out with some facial expressions, known as reflexive smiles, but the smile we give when we're happy or amused? That's something we learn by observing people around us and linking positive experiences—like being held or spoken to or sung "Baby Shark" to—with smiling.

And then, when baby us does smile, we often receive positive feedback: high-pitched squeals, summons to other family members to come over to see this, a flash photo in our face from our caregivers, which reinforces the behavior. Over time we babies learn that smiling is a way to elicit positive attention, so we smile more frequently and link that expression with positive emotions and social interactions. With time and practice (and unspoken but very felt pressure), we become adept at *intentionally socially smiling*. Even if we are sick of "Baby Shark."

Not the case with wholeness.

There's no *Aww, honey, come here! Come here quickly. Little Bobby is having a meaningful moment. Come see his face! He looks so eudaimonic!*

To complicate matters further, we can't even use hedonic-happiness bread crumbs to lead us to eudaimonia. Because, humorously, some of our most profound sources of self-actualization don't produce instant boosts in happiness.

Like having kids—a hallmark of a fulfilling life, yet one that is famously associated with lower levels of happiness (and, I infer, higher incidents of curse words muttered under one's breath). This is known as the "parenthood paradox," which explains that parents often report that while they feel a deep sense of inner purpose while raising children, they outwardly score very, *very* low on measures of happiness. This is perfectly stated by the book title *All Joy and No Fun* by Jennifer Senior, in which she writes, "Children strain our everyday lives . . . but also deepen them. . . . Parents with children at home experience more highs, as well as more lows, than those without children." She references social scientist William Doherty, who calls parenting "a high-cost/high-reward activity."

Another high-cost/high-reward activity is traveling, which is often a very stressful, expensive, challenging, uncomfortable, IBS-triggering event, yet one that deeply enriches our lives. (Which is why my favorite part of a trip is hindsight.)

Arguing, too, is something researchers tie to living a meaningful existence. This is because, as Smith writes in *The Power of Meaning*, "Researchers said [it] was an indication of having convictions and ideals you're willing to fight for." Which fits the bill of how Aristotle defined eudaimonia: as "'seeking to use and develop the best in oneself' in a way that fits with 'one's deeper principles.'"

Because what essentially tips our scales toward more of a deeply eudaimonic life than a jolly "happy" life across the board is connecting to life beyond one's self. Happy feelings can come from what we think of as self-care: having little stress, good physical health, and the ability to do a spur-of-the-moment Target haul without feeling a heavy financial burden. An easy life, in other words. Lots of hedonic vibes.

The eudaimonic flavor of meaningfulness is found more in the exhausting yet purposeful stuff we're told to take self-care breaks FROM.

Ultimately, there's a tension between things that make us happy in the short term and things that offer us fulfillment in the long term. Feeling good, being healthy, and having an easy life make you happy, but don't necessarily give you a life of deep purpose.

So if we can't rely on smiles or pleasurable sensations to tell us if we're living eudaimonically, what are some other options?

Contentment hypothesis

A few years ago, organizational psychologist Adam Grant published a viral article titled "There's a Name for the Blah You're Feeling: It's Called Languishing" in *The New York Times*, in which he suggested that languishing "may be the dominant emotion of 2021."

He described languishing as "the absence of well-being" and "not functioning at full capacity." *Languishing* brings to mind wilting, weakening, hunching over in utter exhaustion. What could better describe the unused slimy spinach in your fridge?

Lying in bed one night, Grant put his finger on an unsettling sense in the air. "It wasn't burnout—we still had energy," he wrote. "It wasn't depression—we didn't feel hopeless. We just felt somewhat joyless and aimless. It turns out there's a name for that: languishing. Languishing is a sense of stagnation and emptiness. It feels as if you're muddling through your days, looking at your life through a foggy windshield."

He added, "In psychology, we think about mental health on a spectrum from depression to flourishing. Flourishing is the peak of well-being: You have a strong sense of meaning, mastery and mattering to others."[16]

That was the first time I heard about this thing called flourishing, but it is a major positive-psychology term. In fact, positive-psych founder Martin Seligman's third book on the topic is called *Flourish*. In it, Seligman reminds readers that positive psychology was not established to be the smiley-face-focused science of happiness it had become known as. "Feeling cheerful or merry is a far cry from what Thomas Jefferson declared that we have the right to pursue," Seligman writes, "and it is an even further cry from my intentions for a positive psychology."

Thus, he declares, "The gold standard for measuring well-being is flourishing."[17]

But still, what does flourishing feel like? We can say it's the opposite of languishing, but that doesn't get us much closer.

If we go back to Finland, we'll notice that the champion of the "happiest country" title has a particularly unique relationship with the sun. During the winter months, the people hardly see it. In the northernmost parts, the sun won't rise above the horizon for anywhere from a few days to several weeks; and in southern Finland, where they get some light, we're talking only a few hours a day. On the flip side, in the summer, the sun pulls all-nighters.

My friend Sloane is a world traveler with over sixty-one countries under her belt. I can hardly keep track of her whereabouts.

"What month did you visit Finland?" I asked her.

"We went in summer, so almost twenty-four hours of sun," she replied, texting some pretty photos my way. "Thinking of going or just reading about Finland because it's always rated the happiest place?"

"Both," I sent back, adding a smiley.

"It's more like they're content," she offered. "They weren't joyful."

"Even better," I thought. And texted.

In 2017, Minna Tervamäki, who was voted Finland's most positive person, told the BBC: "I have very contradictory feelings about the happiness survey. Finnish people read it and laugh, like, 'What? Us?' What comes to my mind is that Finnish people are content more than happy."

Sloane told me, "When we were there, a couple commented on how we must be Americans because we were laughing and smiling for pictures. And that seemed like a sad comment coming from the 'happiest country.'"

Maybe the so-called happiness we yearn for is better characterized as contentment. Contentment may be the closest descriptive feeling of eudaimonia we have in English.

It's kind of like how I'll tell my hairdresser that I want to go "lighter," but I show her eight photos of it *brighter*, so she makes it *brighter* because she knows that's what I actually want. Or it's like when you tell your husband, who's chronically late, that we have to leave at nine o'clock when we actually don't need to leave until nine thirty. I think we say we want "happiness," but those who *are* actually happy know that it's contentment they're feeling, which we think is "happy."

To award a country the "happiest" title, the World Happiness Report sifts through Gallup polls that ask respondents to rate their life satisfaction on a scale from 0 to 10, with 10 being the best possible life. The report doesn't give weight to someone's level of joy and quantity of smiles, but rather, it evaluates the gap between one's life circumstances and their expectations. If one's expectations for a good life closely align with their actual life, happiness (according to the World Happiness Report people) ensues. In other words, the World Happiness Report also believes the greater the gappy, the more unhappy!

But this idea of matching expectations to reality isn't as much a formula for happiness as much as it is the makeup of contentment.

Contentment comes from the Latin *contentus*, which translates to "satisfied" or "contained." *Contentus* described someone who was contained within certain limits yet found satisfaction within those boundaries. Like an indoor cat.

Many philosophical and religious traditions throughout history have molded their own definitions. Stoicism is the ancient Greek form of contentment, which emphasized the importance of finding inner peace and tranquility by accepting the natural order of the universe. Eastern philosophies such as Buddhism and Hinduism regard contentment as an essential characteristic to reach spiritual enlightenment and break free of suffering. According to these teachings, it's important to let go of future desires and embrace contentment in the now.

Contentment is commonly seen as a virtue among Christians, too, where having enough is more important than striving for more wealth and status. In his letter to the Philippians, the apostle Paul wrote: "I have learned to be satisfied in any situation."

In Jewish tradition, the word is *s'machut*, which derives from the Hebrew word meaning "to rejoice" or "to be glad." *S'machut* conveys a sense of inner joy, happiness, and satisfaction. When saying it out loud, one's mouth naturally makes a contented, sly smile.

The happy Nordic countries have their own similar word, *lagom*, which roughly means "just the right amount." It's an overarching ethos that promotes intentional restraint from extravagance. "Similar to hygge in Denmark, lagom is frequently thought to capture the essence of Swedish culture," Danish writer and professor Jukka Savolainen wrote in *Slate*. "In terms of expectations for a good life, lagom encourages contentment with life's bare necessities. If you already have those, you have nothing to complain about. Ergo, you are happy."

Living the lagom life prevents people from having sky-high expectations, instead of chasing the American dream, which says, "The sky's the limit!" and normalizes discontent until you get it, make it, become it.

Complacency

"I believe contentment is really the *happiness* we pursue," I texted Sloane.

"Scott always thinks content sounds like settling," Sloane wrote back, referencing her brother, who is also my friend. "Which I kind of see."

"You think contentment is settling?" I challenged.

"Not fully but there seems to be a touch of that," she replied. "Maybe it's how we use it colloquially."

She's right. Colloquially, people speak of contentment like

it's shameful. Being content is the opposite of being driven, like a slacker who's perfectly fine with just being mediocre, lacking the burning desire that supposedly defines the American spirit of ambition. Where's the hunger?

Well, I was only content at my job, so I searched for something else.

I don't know why your baby's so content just sitting there and not eager to crawl.

Honestly, I'm quite content with my home's landscaping, thank you very much.

What kind of freak isn't actively seeking growth, change, or improvement? What lunatic doesn't have the last five pounds to shed?!

We worry that if we settle with contentment, we're doing something wrong. There's not enough struggle. But pursuing doesn't go with content. You don't pursue contentment. The verb does not work with that noun. You settle into content; you find contentment. You *strive* for happiness, but you *embrace* contentment. Give it a big hug.

But that's not enough for those of us who have been taught by the ghost of Ben Franklin that we "will find the key to success under the alarm clock," that the American dream will come because of diligence, perseverance, and grueling workdays. "It is the working man who is the happy man. It is the idle man who is the miserable man" is another coffee-mug quote Ben wrote. So no shit we fear being idle.

But when I left my graduate program and spent my pregnancy reading existentialism books and trying to stomach dry cereal, I felt an intense sense of satisfaction that I'd never experienced before. I had so much appreciation that I was able to be creating a brand-new human being inside of me, but the predominant reason I was so content lying horizontally and nauseous on my couch was because my self-expectations had been canceled. For the first time in my life, I could be idle.

Limitations liberate us. As Oliver Burkeman writes in *Four Thousand Weeks*, "Once you become convinced that something you've been attempting is impossible, it's a lot harder to keep on berating yourself for failing."

That's exactly what being pregnant did for me. Being forced/freed to lower my expectations for myself meant that I wasn't judging a day by my output or succumbing to pressure for socialization. (Or calling myself a loser for feeling like a trip to UPS was out of the cards that day.)

In an interview with Burkeman on her podcast, *Pulling the Thread*, Elise Loehnan said, "I was a magazine editor in New York for a decade before I moved to Los Angeles. And I remember the relief that I felt in Los Angeles because of the traffic and that there was suddenly a limiting factor on time. Which I know sounds insane. But in New York, there was . . . no valid excuse from work to drinks, to dinner, to drinks, home. I mean, I had no children and I wasn't married. . . . And then when you get to LA and you're like, well, I'm not crossing the 405 at 6:00 P.M. . . . . Suddenly, I was like, I have so much more time by virtue of the fact that I can't actually physically do this. . . . I found it very, very liberating."[18]

Dropping the shackles of expectations is a borderline spiritual experience. There was *no chance* I could continue at the pace I'd been going. I had a legitimate excuse to appreciate the present moment without constantly stoking an inner fire to chase after bigger goals. I had freedom. I gave myself permission to walk, not run, in all aspects of my life. I also—critically— took a social media hiatus. The internet is expectation quicksand. I knew that it would be better for my mental health and newfound sense of contentment to rewatch all seasons of

Dexter and read Sartre. Anytime I did open up Instagram, I saw moms running all over the place. Sometimes literally. I know someone who told her husband she was pregnant after completing a marathon. She ripped off her bib and, underneath her shirt, it read "Running for two!" That's amazing, but who can compete?

This is why the internet is expectation quicksand. The only contentment we see on social media is curated contentment. Aspirational contentment. A contentment aesthetic. Posting to social media requires a certain level of innate showmanship and craftsmanship, and contentment content falls into two categories:

First is the "I'm so at peace with my messy house and dirty kiddos and stretch marks I'll zoom in so you can believe me that they exist because I'm real like you!" performative contentment that can trigger guilt and shame in us about not *also* feeling so at peace with our visible-from-down-the-road stretch marks.

Second is the "I'm just appreciating the simple joy of a beautiful sunset off the balcony at my Aruba hotel" that is simply a humblebrag that gives us an inferiority/dissatisfaction cocktail with a little paper umbrella.

Although I wish it were possible, *contentment* is a hard word to rally around. I can't be out there campaigning for a *contentment*-definition revolution, nor can I definitely change your ingrained understanding of the word in just a few paragraphs. Even my *own* instinct when I hear the word is shame and an image of a well-worn and a little torn brown leather La-Z-Boy recliner, until I remind myself that by *contentment*, what I really mean is SATISFIED.

6

. . . .

Satisfaction Guaranteed

Decision-making is at the heart of existentialism. It's a philosophy whose focus is on the freedom we each have to create our lives with our choices. If nothing binds you or tells you what to do, then it tracks that nobody but you is responsible for what you do. What's more, what you do is important—your actions have consequences. You can try to dodge responsibility, of course, and say that something else is controlling your actions, but over time, no matter what, the things you do (and don't do—which still count!) are adding up and creating who you are.

We need to distinguish existentialism from self-help here, because the stress on personal responsibility can sound similar to self-help's encouragement to take charge of one's own life.

Now, I'm not a doctor, but I am noticing a correlation between our freedom becoming more and more dizzying and depression and anxiety skyrocketing. It almost seems like every new television streaming service with an influx of entertainment to flip between sends a certain percentage of our population over the edge.

This is where satisficing becomes lifesaving.

Satisficing is a word I came across in *The Paradox of Choice* by Barry Schwartz, which I then learned is a remix of an older word that American scientist and Nobel laureate Herbert Simon introduced in 1956. It's a word that describes a non–La-Z-Boy content person. Someone who can stay on SiriusXM's Pop2K channel for an entire car ride without feeling anxious that they may be missing out on some great jams over at Mosaic or the Pulse. It's someone who can soundly rest their head on their pillow at night in acceptance that their day was "good enough."[1]

This person is a satisficer. And I believe that growing into one is fundamental to living eudaimonically. Because satisficing helps us make decisions. And a life of meaning is a life of deciding.

To be able to satisfice is to be comfortable making satisfactory decisions. It's feeling all good with an option that's "good enough," versus ruminating over whether you've chosen the unequivocally best possible option. (Which would be impossible to know unless you tried every single option and evaluated, and we do not have time to test-drive every single car in the lot—and copy and paste that metaphor for potential partners.) It's contrary to our natural inclination, which is fueled by a combination of our cultural programming, which shames us for "settling," and our advertising industry, which crafts smart ways to covertly stir up our dissatisfaction.

"WHAT-IFS" BACKGROUND NOISE

Knowing that *maybe* that other moisturizer is THE ONE can gnaw at us unknowingly. I'm pretty sure I'm balancing thirty-seven what-ifs cycling around the back of my mind at once. *What if I should've gotten a sling bag instead of a fanny pack?! What if I picked that other school for my child?* Every winter, I have a mini existential breakdown about why we live in the Northeast when there are other parts of the world where the weather is sunny and incredible, like a dream year-round.

To quell my angst, I look at all the other people who also live like this. I observe people shoveling their driveway or sweeping up their dead leaves. I share small talk in the street about how cold it is or how gray it is or how it's finally nice but, oops, now it's a little too hot to live somewhere with no cooling coastal breeze. And these little interactions make me feel less like I'm a fool for not living on a beach in Hawaii like I see on social media.

And then I'll stop and think about what my life would actually look like if I moved to Hawaii: I wouldn't be near my small and tight family. I do like cozy snow days, and autumn is the shit. And I would miss hot matchas. Iced all the time isn't the same. So the only way to really calm myself down from these longings is to intentionally sit and think about each one. But that's a lot of work to do on a minute-to-minute basis. Which is what it takes when we get these alternative realities literally every time we open our phone.

Having too many options doesn't just turn us into pickier people; it makes us feel significantly less satisfied with whatever option we choose. In *The Paradox of Choice*, Schwartz talks about going jeans shopping for the first time in about twenty years. (Respect.) He was stunned to experience the vast amount of customization that had transpired since his last denim expedition. Even though Barry is an older man, I couldn't have related harder to this. If it's not going to the Gap to spiral over different inseams, lengths, stretches, and cuts, it's having online shopping paralysis. I recently wanted to buy my first pair of Hoka sneakers, which are all the rage. I honest to god put more time and energy into bouncing between the different options of those sneakers than I put into choosing the ob-gyn who would deliver my baby. After many hours, open browser tabs, and reviews, I got so overwhelmed and exhausted that I ended up abandoning my cart, giving up my 15 percent discount code, and going to AN ACTUAL RUNNING SHOE STORE to get a human's help. And even now when I go for runs or walks in my Hokas, which I love, there's a part of me that wonders, *What if . . . ? Would I love my Hokas even more in another model? With another height or cut or cushion or color?*

As Schwartz writes in *The Paradox of Choice,* "Presenting people with a wide array of options doesn't liberate them: it paralyzes them. If people overcome this paralysis and choose from the large set of options, they are less satisfied with their choice than they would have been if their options had been more limited." But along with that inner set of guidelines, we also have to have tolerance and acceptance for contentment. Without accepting *good enough,* you'll be stuck looking at Hokas forever.

In just one minute on my social media feed, I'll see twenty different haircuts that all look fabulous on twenty different ladies. And one sec, I really want long hair—until the next minute when I see someone rocking short hair. Maybe this is because it has become so much easier than ever to make changes, which actually makes it harder to make choices.

It's easier than ever to try, get, return, and resell just about anything. We can experiment with hair extensions and temporary false eyelashes, rent clothes, and abuse free trials for workouts, meditation apps, TV, and meal subscriptions. Experimenting is much more accessible. Decisions are much less permanent. It used to be that if you bought a refrigerator, you couldn't return it. You technically could, but it'd be a major production to figure out (without the internet) how to disassemble it, load it into the back of your car, and lug it to Sears. Now we can get a customized mattress dropped off in a box, open it, sleep on it for 120 days, and if we don't like it, they'll come pick it up at our door while we're sipping from a mug of our subscription-bagged coffee.

So we live in a land of choices. And a lot of that creates stress. But a lot of that is good, because we can quit, we can pivot, we can move. Whereas owning a house used to be a very permanent thing, now, if we're over it, we can Airbnb our casa, buy an Airstream and a dog, and spend a year living off the grid. That's cool. You don't need to pick a company or career and stay with it for life. And that's a positive, in the way that we can try on so many lives! And if they don't suit us, we can drop out of school, do a different school, change our major, return our refrigerator. But at some point, we have to make a decision or we'll never be happy and always be exhausted.

And so the problem is that this constant state of flux breeds a never-ending cycle of doubt, as everything is always open to change, forcing us to continually question and reevaluate every decision.

Ultimately, though, our underlying angst stems from how hard it is to reckon with the fact that we have only one life. And in our one life, we have endless haircuts we could wear, just like there are endless spouses we could have, and each spouse and haircut would provide completely different life paths. It's baffling if you zoom out and think about it: every decision we make, every day, leads us to one of infinite directions.

While Americans believe more freedom is better, existentialists argue that more freedom equals more angst. "The anguish of freedom is felt when we realize that we are solely responsible for our choices," wrote Camus.

And this is why, as Schwartz writes, "learning how to satisfice is an important step not only in coping with a world of choice, but in simply enjoying life." Being able to experience contentment means you can live in and enjoy this world—not get lost in the despair of the hypothetical. Because to be a satisficer means to make decisions based on what satisfies *you*, and not be disturbed by the residual worry about other possibilities. Be content and carry on.

So, how does one satisfice?

One satisfices by having clear-cut criteria.

Let's go back to the fro yo.

If I were a satisficer, I would walk into the frozen yogurt shop as calm as the chimes above the door. After grabbing the same cup as always, I'd head toward the row of gleaming machines, each containing a different flavor. But I wouldn't get lost surveying the vast array. Instead, I'd walk with determination to my usual machine, and with the precision of an archer, I'd pull down the lever.

Moving on to the toppings, I'd cruise through dangerous territory by knowing what I love: Oreo crumbles, chocolate chips, a couple of Reese's Pieces, and decorative rainbow sprinkles.

Onlookers would look on, mesmerized, spoons half hanging out their open mouths. My confidence would shine like a beacon. I'd carry my masterpiece to the cashier, who'd marvel at my swift and decisive selection.

"I've never seen anyone navigate the toppings bar so effortlessly!" she would exclaim.

I'd lean in and whisper, "You see, knowing your tastes and preferences helps you become a superhero in everyday life. It's about being confident in the choices we make, knowing what brings us joy."

She would nod as this wisdom washed over her. "By understanding our own tastes, preferences, and desires," I'd continue, "we empower ourselves to make decisions that truly align with our authentic selves."

Satisficing is all about making decisions as quickly as possible to keep decision fatigue at bay. To do that, we have to move away from our easy time-suck fixation of finding the absolute perfect choice and instead be cool with something that satisfies our predetermined criteria. Thinking about personal values provides a sense of direction, allowing for decisions that bring greater satisfaction and less angst.

But values can be a tricky topic, because they can seem heavy and nuanced, plus a little pretentious. But they're basically the stuff that you, personally, determine are important.

You could call these your fucks. A bunch of popular books use the concept of "choose where you give your fucks" as a simile for what's worthy of your emotional energy and literal time. In his bestselling book *The Subtle Art of Not Giving a F*ck*, Mark Manson uses *fuck* to mean things we care about or give importance to in our lives. He tells us to discover what few things are important enough for us to give a fuck about, and then flip the bird to all the other stuff, which he calls "pointless distractions." He says that not separating fucks from no fucks is causing us to spread ourselves too thin, trying to derive pleasure from too many things.[2] Similarly, for Sarah Knight in *her* bestselling book, *The Life-Changing Magic of Not Giving a F*ck*, the f-bomb represents our mental energy and emotional investment that we choose to allocate or withhold based on our priorities and values.[3]

Values are the beliefs and attitudes that guide our behavior.

They're like our own personal set of rules; a way of talking about what's important to us and how we live our lives. Our values are constantly being reflected in the way we choose to behave—every moment, when we're deciding what to give our attention, where to direct our energy, how to spend our time, "give our fucks," we're making value-laden decisions. Your behavior tag-teams your values.

"To fight the powerful influence that the constant bombardment of advertising has on your life ideals, you need an even more powerful inner compass," modern philosopher Frank Martela writes in *A Wonderful Life*. "You need to have some self-chosen values and life goals that are so strong and salient that you can retain your integrity even in an advertisement-filled society."[4]

We could also break values into two categories: core values and secondary values. Core values are fundamental principles that guide our lives and are typically very broad. They're the stuff that sounds great as a mission statement on a company's "About Us" page. Innovation. Collaboration. Curiosity.

Secondary values are more specific and individualized. They reflect our personal preferences, tastes, and priorities, which are based on our unique interests, experiences, personalities, and cultural backgrounds. Since we change over time, so can they! These are "country music" values, enjoying the little things in life, like fishing in the dark, flatbed trucks, and chicken that is fried.

Like we "vote with our dollars," we create our life with our secondary values. Every decision we make—big, medium, or small—results from saying, "I choose this over that." It's a choice to blow off Mom's birthday to do sake bombs with the popular kids because they finally invited you. It's a decision to do yoga rather than watch the latest popular TV show and suffer not being able to talk about it at the office. Because values are always being weighed against one another to create our decisions, their spots in our personal hierarchy are always migrating.

I love how Dr. Russ Harris, an Australian psychotherapist, describes values in relation to the continents on the globe. "No matter how fast you spin that globe," Harris says, "you can never see all the continents at once; there are always some at the front, some at the back. From moment to moment, you get to choose: which values come to the front, and which move to the back?"[5]

This means we must decide what choices in our lives really, *really* matter, and focus our time and energy there. This also means we will naturally forgo some things, but we will enjoy the things we choose even more.

This may sound like lowering expectations for our life, but I think it's more like accepting life's finitude. In our culture, it's taboo to discuss life having limits. Life, if our parents raise us right, is supposed to be limitless! But this causes "existential overwhelm," which Oliver Burkeman explores in his book, writing, "The modern world provides an inexhaustible supply of things that seem worth doing, and so there arises an inevitable and unbridgeable gap between what you'd ideally like to do and what you actually can do."[6]

The solution is inherently existentialish: it's accepting the reality that our time is limited, and within that, every second of every day we are fully free and responsible for our actions. But rather than this making us so elated that we want to run around streaking while binge-eating pizza because FREEDOM, Sartre believed this causes us great anguish. Because even though we are free to make our life whatever we want by the choices we make, we cannot live a life that is both as a mom and childless. We can't be a kindergarten teacher, an anesthesiologist, and a vegan pastry chef all in a day's work. We can't simultaneously live in Hawaii, in Croatia, and on a small island in Maine. We can't be an Orthodox Jew and a Buddhist monk, nor can we root for the Red Sox AND the Yankees. It's awfully overwhelming to accept full responsibility for the choices we make. If we can even *make* a decision. Which is why you might recognize some of our most common decision-paralysis relief strategies:

Let Jesus (or Zuckerberg) take the wheel

It used to be that religion was where we turned for help making choices. For millennia, religious leaders were our trustworthy experts. We'd go to their houses of worship in hopes of finding the keys to a happy life in a sermon, a song, or a scribble on a bathroom-stall door. They were a one-stop shop for help with all of life's happenings, guiding us literally from birth to death and answering questions about existing in between. I've known people who go to their rabbis for help with party planning, grief, marriage counseling, circumcisions, alcoholism, and referrals for chiropractors who specialize in post-hoisting-groom-in-chair-at-wedding back pain.

And I've never sought guidance from a priest, but if television is any indication, it seems like they, too, get desperate inquiries for help with the angst of being alive. In her show *Fleabag*, Phoebe Waller-Bridge laments to her priest: "I want someone to tell me what to wear in the morning. I want someone to tell me what to wear *every* morning. I want someone to tell me what to eat. What to like, what to hate, what to rage about, what to listen to, what band to like, what to buy tickets for, what to joke about, what not to joke about. I want someone to tell me what to believe in, who to vote for, who to love and how to tell them. I just think I want someone to tell me how to live my life, Father, because so far I think I've been getting it wrong. And I know that's why people want people like you in their lives, because you just tell them how to do it."

Once upon a time, regardless of one's faith, places of worship gave us structure, rules, and limits before we ever thought to ask for them. That helped us, for better or worse, make decisions. But today, Americans are leaving religious institutions in droves. According to a 2021 Pew Research report, almost a third of adults in the United States are now "nones."[7] Not to be confused with *nuns*, *nones* is an all-encompassing term for people who reject religious affiliation. Nones are a mixed bag of atheists, agnostics, and "(c) None of the above." And as the fastest-growing segment of America's religious landscape, *none*-ing is taking off.

Without religious institutions, our search for two of the most important components of happiness/meaning and belonging has to be intentional and deliberate. It also requires courage and creativity.

Because if we don't frequent houses of worship, there's no relying on a divine meet-cute with our future spouse at Sunday school. There's no hope of meshing with a squad of like-minded friends on a mission trip. This is a predicament many Americans are finding themselves in today.

Countless books and articles talk about our existential uncertainty and angst rising in conjunction with the rising rejection of organized religion. Because if we were skipping sermons because of a craving to Chipotle-burrito-bowl-build our own unique spiritual-guidance system, that is our prerogative, which is awesome. Less awesome, however, is that most of us aren't replacing the religious hole in our hearts with anything that causes us to look inward.

This is problematic because ingrained in us humans is a

capacity to ruminate, reflect, think back, forecast ahead, and *deeply* process what it means when we see a black limousine driving slowly down a street with a trail of cars tightly behind it, running red lights . . .

We are constantly confronted with our mortality. We recognize that life is uncertain. We understand that pain and sorrow and loss are part of our destiny. We know that we and our loved ones will age and pass away. And while each David Attenborough nature documentary shows us that lions and leopards also know that death is a thing that looms, we humans need to make more sense of it than "life goal: eat and don't get eaten." We have an insatiable inner requirement to know what the point of all this is. And if we phase out religion, which most of us are doing, we're cutting ourselves off from parables that offer potential existential explanations and people that offer community and connection. This means more and more of us are living without a designated space to discuss values and be offered spiritual strategies to guide us. So, to make meaning out of our life, we are really left to our own devices.

Literally.

Instead of finding wisdom in religious elders citing old scriptures, we have influencers writing new captions. We're using the chaos of social media to scratch our itches for meaning, connection, and belonging. Questions that we used to take to our religious congregations—like *How do I live a life that I like?*—are now questions an algorithm serves up our answers to. Because even as technology advances, the baseline need to ease our existential angst doesn't budge.

And it's not just internet advice-givers who get on their little square soapboxes and offer life guidance via astrological memes, fifteen-second self-quiz reels, and deeply revelatory personal mini-essays below a captivating image—every picture we see on social media is from somebody communicating what's important to them. (Or communicating what they think ought to be important to them.) We're absorbing *their* secondary values. Either their honest ones (unlikely) or the values they think we think they have.

The sociologist Charles Horton Cooley coined the concept of the looking-glass self, according to which, who we are is based on how we interact with others. In fact the opinions of other people influence our own identity. He wrote about this back in 1902 when we socialized in person, and I'm amused by the irony that as it applies today to our socialization by media, it's essentially saying that social media influencers influence *us* by using an identity that is influenced *by* us. Our looking-glass self basically decides our online presence. Our content is influenced by our audience.

Our looking-glass self can majorly impact our behavior on social media. When we post, we usually consider how our content will be seen by others and how it could shape their opinion of us. Essentially, this means that on social media, we're just recycling the same societal values and standards . . . about our appearance, way of life, success, and other matters.

I think depression and suicide are skyrocketing because most people are in an existential crisis right now. No one knows what the fuck gives them meaning. Because we're told and shown on Instagram, if you swipe up and buy this, this will give you meaning. If you join me at this, this will give you purpose. No one knows what secondary values exist inside of them, *because everyone is just looking at what everyone else is doing and copying and pasting their lives.*

Why would an appearance making spaghetti on *Good Morning America* be more worth celebrating than, say, teaching a group of new parents what to do in case their baby is choking? Or giving a cancer survivor his first post-remission haircut? Or hanging up my wet towel after use for a full week straight?

Because that's what we see. Philosophers since the time of the ancient Greeks have been concerned about the human proclivity toward distraction. Their chief concern has been the fact that our attention defines our reality.

We feel like all that's worthy of a post on our Facebook walls are the once-a-year humungo milestones, because that's what we see, when, really, a good life, the eudaimonic life, is what happens *in between* the splashy milestones for which Party City has a ready-made celebratory balloon.

This in-between time that we just throw away or disregard or think is unnoteworthy is what comedian Jerry Seinfeld once referred to as "garbage time." In an interview, he said, "I'm a believer in the ordinary and the mundane. These guys that talk about 'quality time'—I always find that a little sad when they say, 'We have quality time.' I don't want quality time. I want the garbage time. That's what I like. You just see them in their room reading a comic book and you get to kind of watch that for a minute, or [having] a bowl of Cheerios at 11 o'clock at night when they're not even supposed to be up. The garbage, that's what I love."[8]

A disregard for garbage time in one's social media highlights is perpetuated by both the voyeur and the poster—both people on either side of the looking glass. We're all keeping this going. Because we both don't celebrate these things and don't ask for them to be celebrated. So if all we grow up seeing on media are these big-kahuna accomplishments, we will think that's what life is all about. Because we think that, we'll also live big-kahuna accomplishment to big-kahuna accomplishment and post nothing but those, too, throwing more and more actually great things into the garbage-time category.

It's tough not to be influenced by what we see.

In general, I feel that we've collectively become a little confused about the word *influence*. I think we use it synonymously with *inspiration*, but that is incorrect. The intended gist of the verb *to influence* is to describe promoting or inducing someone to do something, to animate them with an idea or purpose! *Inspire* is a relative to the Latin word *inspirare*, which means to figuratively breathe upon someone. There's a lifting-up energy to the word. An image of lifting a bird out of my hands comes to mind. Fly, little birdie, fly! Or whipping your hands out of a team huddle "Break!" after all hands were in. *On three. One, two, three, team!* But the only hand involvement with *inspire* on Instagram is using our hands to swipe and double tap. It seems we're having a tricky time telling the difference between "inspire" and "make you think your life isn't good enough."

Follow signs

Another way we outsource the decision-making overwhelm is by giving power to signs, so we're not just out here trying to navigate life like lone rangers. Sometimes it's just helpful to get some clues as to where we should set up camp. And where to set up camp, it turns out, is one of the most "show me a sign!" life activities for us; I have met approximately no one who didn't have at least a *twinge* of magic involved in the story of finding their home. I am no exception.

When we feel lost in life and stuck deciding, getting insight from an unbiased friend like The Universe can be a tremendous help. As Camus once said, "In the face of the enormity of the world's chaos, the only freedom we have is how we choose to respond to it." So since the beginning of time, we've devised decision rituals to help us make choices in the face of the enormity of the world's chaos—incorporating elements of chance, symbolism, personal beliefs, and plastic.

There's coin flipping, which the Romans originally called coin tossing. Instead of "tail," they used "ship," and for "head," well, they also used "head." There's the Magic 8 Ball, a pool-ball-shaped choice maker that has a floating twenty-sided die inside with a little window to show the die's responses to yes or no questions. Tarot cards are artful card decks wherein each card has its own special meaning and symbolic interpretation that only the tarot reader can decipher and apply to one's quandary. Of course, there's also Rock Paper Scissors, the only decision-maker that doesn't require a prop. While its exact origins are unclear, the first mention of this hand game dates back to the Han dynasty. While the weapons have varied throughout years and cultures (in its earliest days it was Frog Slug Snake; then later a fox got involved; and some cultures play with weapons like bears, water, elephants, and ants), the method of using a random draw of hand gestures to decide for us has been a helpfully fair choosing method between two parties.

Ultimately, we will give away our agency to an inanimate object because the damn burden of responsibility is so uncomfortable. This was proved by science! In a study by a researcher at the University of Chicago, people who were struggling to make an important decision in their life, like leaving a job or a relationship, were instructed to flip a coin. More people than not followed the coin's advice and changed their decision if the coin signified them to, *and* six months later, those who followed the flip of the coin said that they were far more settled with their decisions than those who ignored the coin's wisdom.[9]

As I said before when "synchronicity" led me to my first self-help book, the notion that things happen for a reason beyond ye ol' standard cause and effect was an idea introduced by Swiss psychologist Carl Jung in 1928.

Jung theorized that some events can be linked by their subjective and personal meaning without a clear, logical explanation. Jung felt that something remarkable was at play when two or more events seemed to be connected in a way that couldn't be chalked up to chance.

> We often dream about people from whom we receive a letter by the next post. I have ascertained on several occasions that at the moment when the dream occurred the letter was already lying in the post-office of the addressee. —C. G. Jung, *Synchronicity: An Acausal Connecting Principle*

Jung thought synchronicity was a sign of something bigger in the world: proof that the universe offers us little clues about our lives and our destiny. Little clues could be as subtle as hearing a forgotten tune on the radio or as strange as déjà vu. For Jung, these coincidences can be a guide.

The thing is, like using tarot cards, interpreting these little synchronicities is subjective. A few years ago, Jesse and I were losing a lot of sleep trying to decide whether to move out of New York City into a house with a lawn and a full kitchen and a septic system, or stay in the city with a superintendent and a trash chute and a front-row seat to the doing and eating epicenter of the world. One day, after a particularly exhausting pro-and-con conference, I went outside for a jog to clear my head. As I always do, I put my running playlist on shuffle (another way we can outsource decision-making!). Of course, the first song that came on was Jay-Z and Alicia Keys's "Empire State of Mind," a song celebrating New York. New York *"will make you feel brand new and inspire you . . ."* In New York, you're unstoppable.

I laughed out loud. *Oh, you sneaky little universe, you!*

But then I paused.

What are you trying to tell me? I asked.

Because I could see this going either way. One reason I wanted to leave New York City was specifically because of those big-city lights *and* all the concrete. Those were on my cons list! Was this a sign to move on out?

Or.

I love how in the city there's nothing I can't do. And I love how it inspires me. Are you telling me to stay?!?!?!

I laughed and realized that synchronicity is always up to interpretation. Rarely is a sign we receive a billboard on the side of the road that reads: "Grow Your Gray Hair Out, Laurie!"

Because we're out here on our own to create meaning out of our big life, we assist ourselves by assigning meaning to little things so they can serve as eggs on this endless existence scavenger hunt.

When Jesse and I eventually decided to move out of New York City, away from the big-city lights, taxis, and subway, I had to reacquaint myself with the driving life, especially at night. Because our house is in the woods where even lowly lit streetlights would ruin our perfect stargazing yards, it is a sea of darkness at night.

Now I was no stranger to dark driving; at my lowest and loneliest in college, I'd drive four hours to and from my dorm to my home on highways every weekend. But after just short of a decade of my letting subway trains take me home, it'd been a while since it was my job to take me home on the pitch-black country roads.

It felt scary when I couldn't see more than like three hundred feet ahead of me. I had to go slowly, follow the white line on the right, and pray a deer didn't leap out in front of me. Famously, the writer E. L. Doctorow once said about writing, "Writing is like driving at night in the fog. You can only see as far as your headlights, but you can make the whole trip that way."[10] When it comes to living, that darkness can swallow you whole. This is why I think we rely on headlights, little hints from the universe that we give meaning to in order to help light our way. Because that's how we, too, can make our whole trip.

Get to inbox zero (distraction)

It's 2003 and Howie Mandel is pacing around Ellen DeGeneres's TV stage. This confuses us viewers, since guests on her talk show typically stride straight to the lux armchair beside her. The crowd giggles, Ellen acts baffled, and Howie keeps his energy nervous and his eyes focused on the watch fastened around his wrist.

"I have to hit a certain number of steps every day," he explains. "And I'm going to be totally honest: I just flew in from New Orleans and I am not even close to the number of steps I need to hit." As he continues weaving figure eights around Ellen, he deadpans, "But that doesn't stop me from doing your show."

We laugh.

"How many [steps] do you have to hit?" Ellen asks.

"I have to hit ten thousand steps," he replies. "And right now, I'm at twenty-three hundred."

We laugh.

"I should walk more, too," Ellen says, as she rises and conducts the rest of their interview playing follow the (bald) leader.

That's what we can all fall into doing, right? Copying others' *should*s? If there's any game from our youth that I'd prefer we take with us as we age, I wish it was the "Why?" game, not Follow the Leader.

Because while it's fun as kids to ask why zebras have stripes and how cotton candy is made, it's essential as grown-ups to ask why we must walk ten thousand steps a day. And why we should get to inbox zero. And why it's smart to channel pre-baby-delivery stress into packing the hospital bag.

Mandel was ahead of his time on that Ellen show stage as he proved how self-monitoring can lead to self-torment. (And also obsessively hand sanitizing before it was government mandated.)

And while watching Howie and Ellen pace around the stage made me laugh so hard it stuck with me for over ten years, it's one of those "truth in comedy" gags because it's completely real that step-trackers can cause people to feel so pressured and unworthy of sleeping with less than 10K steps under their feet, which is why they've made pj's that look more like street clothes.

Some have called this the "Quantified Self" movement—the notion that we can gain self-knowledge by obsessively tracking ourselves like we're both a lion *and* our prey. We could also call this the "look at metrics instead of my inner self" distraction method.

Whereas I once needed to manually tally how many birthday posts I got on my Facebook wall to determine if I was loved or not, the app does it for me. When my doctor would ask how many hours I typically sleep, I'd pause and do mental math (plus some finger counting) to give her an answer. It used to be that the idea of knowing how many hours I stood in a day was absurd, and that the only way for my mom to know how many hours I'd pissed away on TV was to lie.

But thanks to a massive uptick in what's known as "wearable technology," I can get a full-scope update on my self-statistics while waiting in line for a salad. And using my "hand-holdable technology," I can quickly see how many missed calls, texts, and emails to dread over, and I can discover an old notification that I missed our friend's birthday and a free food-delivery voucher that has now expired.

But all this, in a sick way, is *"better?"* than facing our actual reality. Our focus on doing can be a way to avoid feeling. While we're pacing around trying to hit 10K steps, we can't also sit and mull over what gives our life meaning and how many steps away we might be from that life. *I'd prefer the shin splints, thank you very much.*

Similar to what my husband does when I hand him my bag to hold while I pee, knowing what to do with all this self-data is befuddling. We may not hold it with the tips of our fingers like it's an explosive device, but I think we do try to find meaning in all these built-in measurements.

Originally the idea was to track health-related matters like steps, sleep, heart rate, push-up reps, mood patterns, fiber consumption, and ovulation data, since the assumption was that knowing this stuff about ourselves would help us thrive. But more recently, it's become easy-peasy to collect data on pretty much *anything* measurable: how many books we've read, movies we've seen, followers we've obtained, minutes we've meditated, sauvignon blancs we've tasted, words we've written, debt we've paid off, hours we've volunteered, kind words we've said to our spouse, old sweaters we've donated . . . And we're encouraged to not scribble these numbers in our modest little diary but instead to show them off like one of those "Tripadvisor Loves Us!"

stickers seen on most restaurants in most tourist towns. Long gone are the days when we showed a little personality by pasting a subtle little family of stick figures or college logos to our rear windshield; now we update our social media profiles with the exact number of road races we've finished or countries we've visited. I'm surprised we don't yet feel called to show off the to-date sum of our charitable donations in our email signature, too.

What I'm getting at is, since we don't really know what to *do* with the final tally of British mystery novels we read in October or the length of time we can hold a plank, we turn our quantitative measurements into competitive sports—displaying them on public scoreboards, enabling us to pit ourselves against one another. This may be due to our friendly competitive nature, but it also may be the world's smartest distraction strategy. A lot of our push for productivity is an elaborate ruse for distraction.

Distraction from what?

Distraction from being alone with our thoughts.

If we're not busy tracking our steps, or logging our workouts, or assessing our social media analytics, we have to be all alone in our head, and distraction is quite a bit easier. A headline of an article in *Science* reads, "People Would Rather Be Electrically Shocked Than Left Alone with Their Thoughts."[11]

Science is not in the satire-writing business. Rather, this headline is referencing the results from a slew of studies conducted by social psychologist Timothy Wilson at the University of Virginia in Charlottesville.

"In 11 studies," says an abstract by Wilson, "we found that participants typically did not enjoy spending 6 to 15 minutes in a room by themselves with nothing to do but think, that they enjoyed doing mundane external activities much more, and that many preferred to administer electric shocks to themselves instead of being left alone with their thoughts."

I'm sorry, what?

It's true. When researchers put participants (mostly college students) alone in a bland, sterile lab room for fifteen minutes, rather than quietly think, hum a song, mentally plan their next vacation, or brainstorm how they might want to reorganize their pantry so they could easily see they already had four cans of garbanzo beans, which would prevent them from buying more, 67 percent of men and 25 percent of women chose to press a button and inflict an electric shock on themselves.

And sure, some of this can be equated to how we're uncomfortable with boredom because of our smartphones, but I could see that more as a reason to pick at your hangnails while you sat in a room for fifteen minutes; inflicting deliberate discomfort seems like something a little more extreme.

I had a hairdresser who once confessed to me, as she splashed water down my smock, that she was exhausted from working way too much. She said that it was really taking a toll on her new relationship with this dude she liked.

The more we got to talking (during a three-hour hair appointment, a lot of secrets get spilled), it started to seem like the causality was reversed. It wasn't that her relationship was deteriorating because she worked too much; it was more like she worked too much because she was afraid to acknowledge she didn't like the new dude.

Classic, us making ourselves too busy to have to be home in our heads.

We also distract ourselves from confronting the deeper questions and problems of existence. As comedian Bill Burr says in his 2012 special, "I think I know how to raise a kid. You know what it is? You just play catch with 'em. I think that's the big deal. That's how you raise a kid. You play catch with 'em. And you just talk about life. You distract 'em by throwing the ball. They don't even notice you're filling their heads up with your theories."[12]

This was the belief of Nietzsche, who wrote about how facing the reality of our mortality can feel unsettling and uncomfortable. He thought that rather than address these difficulties and challenges of life head-on, we distract ourselves by filling our time with meaningless activities like playing catch and superficial pleasures like entertainment.

Since Nietzsche's heyday of writing was in the late nineteenth century, his ideas of "entertainment" distractions may have looked slightly different from ours today, but losing ourselves in *Emily in Paris* and YouTube makeup tutorials and competing with our work BFF for most daily steps walked, I believe he would agree, are all part of a self-ruse to forget about our freaky mortality reality.

"We labour at our daily work more ardently and thoughtlessly than is necessary to sustain our life," Nietzsche wrote, "because to us it is even more necessary not to have leisure to stop and think. Haste is universal because everyone is in a flight from himself."[13]

Today, "our daily work" encompasses way more than where we are employed. Our "daily work" can be anything and everything we can tally, track, or time. Most of us put a hell of a lot of effort into not facing reality. Realizing this is our one and only life and that it's up to *us* to make it meaningful can really stir up our emotions, but somehow those worries disappear when trying to hit those 2,500 more steps.

Distraction is a common existentialist stance on what the heck we do with ourselves all day. So much of life is us distracting ourselves from hard truths. In a way, life is one big coping mechanism.

7

. . . .

Self Is a Verb

So this was supposed to be the "Be Yourself" chapter. Since we already covered breaking free of the blueprints of self-help, forgetting trying to be Normal°, and creating your life from one value-based choice at a time, it was now going to be like, *Let's go! You're free! Be you! Go live self-loyally!*

But as I was living this story in real time, I learned something really disappointing (you got me again, expectationists!): there is no grand SELF to ta-da and reveal like a high-level performance of peekaboo. I envisioned that after I shed all the bullshit, I would be left with the *real* me to live the rest of my life with. I could confidently bring this *real* me to weddings, the mall, and the small cheese shop in town!

No. It turns out that such thinking is yet *another* belief system perpetuated by the self-improvement army. According to my research, approximately 89.7342 percent of quotes about authenticity out there pair the word *embrace* with *your authentic self* like we pair a chilled brut rosé and a sunny patio. It's all self, self, self. Singular. Be yourself. Love yourself. Embrace your authentic self. So no wonder I assumed there was a true self waiting for me to welcome, and then love, and then live.

But this isn't so. There is no static self. And attempting to define a fixed self is like trying to determine the absolutely correct way to eat a taco. No. Rather, from the existentialist viewpoint, a self is more like something we *do*—it's active instead of passive. Self is a verb.

Maintaining your sense of self requires actively scrutinizing the accepted facts and truths of life. It's making sure that you didn't receive a side of desires from society that was actually meant for the couple at table 7. Being a self is constantly checking to ensure you don't have any unwanted societal values stuck to the bottom of your foot like toilet paper.

Our self is like a living organism within us, which we nourish by constantly undergoing a process of introspection.

It's around the topic of selfhood in particular where the philosophical ideas of existentialism shine brightest. Because existentialists are our bluntly honest friends who tell us that, yes, our butt does look weird in those pants, but they also don't shy away from telling us that our precious self that we hold so dear is only a concept—it's just the sum of what we've done in life so far.

Our culture has us falsely believing that there's a fixed self inside us that we must discover like we're on a scavenger hunt. Or, really, it's more like life is advertised as one big tough mudder race, and self-help guides and their step-by-step books, programs, and coaching all exist to teach us to crawl in the mud under the 10,000-volt electric wire, or dunk in the 34-degree ice pit, or scale the 40-foot floating net ladder that all stand between us and our coveted core self—and a free T-shirt.

I love how author Gish Jen describes our culture's model of

self as an avocado.[1] She says that we're taught that there's a pit inside of us. And that pit is our self, our essence, our identity— the thing for which we feel we must above all be true.

To me, housing an avocado pit within seems to imply that our self is predetermined—the fleshy green healthy fat grows *around* the pit center—and there's not much of a creative collaboration between us and it. Sure, of course we can individuate ourselves by what clubs we join at school, what side we want with which kind of burger cooked how well, if we prefer our nails filed round or square, but these customizations are how we make ourselves a unique individual only within certain parameters.

The key is the parameters. Let's call these parameters "cultural expectations."

We're encouraged to make ourselves unique under the enormous umbrella of our cultural expectations. *Pick what you enjoy doing to become successful, but you want to be successful, right? Red shutters or blue shutters? Obviously you want a big, beautiful house, but you get to pick the shutters! What diet and/or exercise plan are you going to dip in and out of in your constant stress about those last five pounds? What's your handle?*

Always Mr. Practical, Jesse explained to me that in college, he took a political science class and the professor said something that really stuck with him. The professor said that in this capitalist world, where we're obsessed with freedom, we pretend, we think, we convince ourselves that deciding *Do I want a BMW or a Mercedes or a Toyota?* is freedom of choice. But truly, they're the same. All cars are the same. And if you think instead of getting an Audi, you get a Subaru and that's you expressing your individuality, they've successfully sold you that lie. A car is a car is a car. It drives. It has a backup camera. It has four seats (usually, at least). It has a trunk. The professor warned about thinking you're expressing your individual freedom just because you're literally choosing.

While we're told that we're free to do whatever we want and that we can fully express ourselves, there are unspoken parameters all around us. It's an illusion of freedom. We're made to believe we're extraordinary and unrestricted but are boxed in with parameters.

This is what I did when I followed the advice of my Guide.

I thought I was being unique by choosing my own Instagram handle. By branding myself something completely creative. By wearing the clothes I chose and the lipstick color that favored my skin tone, etc., etc., etc. But all I was doing was customizing myself within the parameters of what my Guide deemed meaningful. Self-help books sell us the same self. If you read one, they're mainly about the same topics: make money, secure love, have a perfect house, take vacations, make passive income. All guides seem to think our true selves are predestined to make passive income. If we follow their advice. Which we pay for. So they make passive income. Boom.

This is the nightmare of following advice. All we're doing is following someone else's values. Unless we're reading a guidebook about a specific skill like artfully layering rugs, or pairing wine with curry, or unclogging a toilet without a plunger, any general "how to be happy" guidebooks are a direct reflection of the author's values. As Thomas Sowell, an American economist and author of twenty-five books, once said, "Politics is the art of making your selfish desires seem like national interest."[2] Substitute "advice" for politics and the point stays the same: self-improvement advice is when you prescribe your desires to everyone. *Cough* Ben *cough cough*.

This is why I believe all advice ought to come with an "IT

DEPENDS!" disclaimer. Like how there's a surgeon general's warning on all boxes of cigarettes, or how in Mexico they put a humongous warning sign on processed foods like chips and candy, I think all guides ought to come with a similar warning: *Attention: Results from following this book's advice may vary depending on your willingness to actually put down the book and take action. Disclaimer: This book may cause a temporary illusion that you have your life figured out. Side effects may include existential crises. Caution: The author is not liable for any awkward moments resulting from the excessive use of self-help jargon in everyday conversations.*

Self for Sale

Offered in the self-improvement menus are the common categories like financial independence, personal happiness, a very lively sex life, and a career that oozes with passion. Self-help books can downplay and restrict your growth by targeting only preset objectives. Urging everyone to aim for the same goals despite their true nature and desires can cause stress, suffering, and what Dr. Gabor Maté calls the "split self":[3] when we feel parts of us are acceptable and other parts are shameful, we adjust accordingly.

Even if we don't read self-help books, we are constantly absorbing messages about the parameters we should try to squeeze ourselves into, like an overstuffed suitcase. I love how Susan Cain talks about the "extrovert ideal" in her book *Quiet.*[4] Starting in the early 1900s, Americans had risen to the richest nation in the world thanks largely to the growth of huge corporations that were selling goods all over the globe. The economic boom yielded a white-picket-fence boom, as families started moving from the country into those suburban art deco homes. This mass migration into houses neatly stacked one next to the other meant that, as Cain writes, "Americans found themselves working no longer with neighbors but with strangers. 'Citizens' morphed into 'employees,' facing the question of how to make a good impression on people to whom they had no civic or family ties."

Basically, as fantastic career opportunities were sprouting up, competition reared its ugly but inevitable head, and it became more and more important to be liked. There was a new Ben Franklin figure leaking his values and ambitions into the tap water of this era. His name was Dale Carnagey—I mean Carnegie, which is what he changed his name to in order to presumably tie himself with the steel magnate Andrew Carnegie, to whom he had no relation. Dale Carnegie is the wealth-driven farm boy turned failed actor turned subpar traveling salesman turned speaking guru who wrote the book *How to Win Friends and Influence People*, which came out in 1936 and is *still* found at airport bookstores and on bestseller lists today. His book could also be called *Charisma for World Domination*, because the gist of Carnegie and his book is "win people with your charming extroverted personality." Funny enough, *charisma* (the word) had been used strictly in a religious sense, meaning a special power gifted to you by God to be put to use for the good of your church. But in 1922, ~~Carnagey~~ Carnegie essentially rebranded charisma to mean having a personal magnetism that you can learn to turn on. No God needed. "You can make more friends in a month by being interested in them than in ten years by trying to get them interested in you," he said, with a sparkle in his eyes. His work, and that of those who piggybacked off him, created a low-key panic in people to master a magnetic personality. Carnegie wanted to turn everyone into a salesman—of themselves.

Selling ourselves is more prevalent today than ever before. We have commercialized our everyday life, turned ourselves into a currency, and made our personality a brand. This magnetic personality Carnegie wanted to help everyone become in the 1920s was like lipstick—something you could apply during the day and wipe off at night. Today, there's no off. Our lips are permanently stained. Just in case we need to snap one of the 93 billion selfies taken *each day*.

While we all know people's "best selves" are what flood our feeds, we don't actually really *know* know. Our cognition, the way we think, is so heavily influenced by the cultural environment around us that it's virtually impossible to know if our true "self" differs from our "selfie" self. Meaning, as social scientist John Hewitt says in Will Storr's book,[5] "I'd say culture is about 90 percent of who we are."

This is a tough pill to swallow. When I first read that, I gagged a little bit. *But I am a unique individual! I do not mold myself to my culture and allow performative influencers to actually influence who I am as a person!* I shouted to Hewitt in my head.

But the joke's on me, because even advocating *that* is culture affecting 90 percent of who I am. In the West, we're so ingrained with the idea that we must strive to be different from others—we're culturally mandated to not be anything less than unique. Rather than just *be* unique, because by default, even like puppies who don't grow up being read bedtime stories about living out their uniqueness, we are naturally genetically, anatomically, astrologically unique. We in the West make being unique an active pursuit. And it's causing a personal brandemic where we're arguably placing more significance on signaling our uniqueness than just living and letting any differences from our neighbors play out naturally, and perhaps subtly.

In a social media culture where we're shown it's possible to straight up turn ourselves into cash cows, the pressure to differentiate grows by every Tik and Tok of the clock. I'm pretty certain that if Camus were here today, he would be tickled by the irony and contradiction of fitting into our social norm of uniqueness by purposely playing up our uniquenesses. It's like how the act of trying to be nonconformist itself becomes a form of conformity. It'd be like joining a club of nonconformists. You know, showing up at a Monday-night meeting with a carton of Dunkin' Donuts coffee and saying, *Hi! I'm John and I'm here to join the Nonconformity Club! What's our agenda?*

Admittedly, when we grow up in a culture that enforces individuation, it becomes hard to parse out what is our natural uniqueness and our performative uniqueness. And this confusion between what's "us" and what is society's imprint on us holds up every generation.

"Every society reproduces its culture—its norms, its underlying assumptions, its modes of organizing experience—in the form of personality," Christopher Lasch writes in *The Culture of Narcissism.*

This is why, according to Cain, a shy child in the 1920s got rebranded as one with a "maladjusted personality," and schools became hyperfocused on teaching students to override any introverted nature and socialize well in order to succeed at life. And then, as soon as personality became a performance, Americans started idolizing charismatic movie stars. (Makes sense.) And as personality became a performance from which we tried to take cues from movie stars, companies started advertising their products as solutions to the anxiety that came with that. My favorite factoid about this rise of the extrovert ideal is how in 1955, antianxiety medications were sold as remedies for the unrelenting anxiety of being judged by others. In 1960, a tranquilizer called Serentil ran an ad that literally said, "For the anxiety that comes from not fitting in."

Oh, how I wish we were still so blunt. Because today we, of course, still have anxiety that comes from not fitting in, yet we do not call it that. Instead, we call it "Hey! Hey! Over here! Do you like this photo of me posing intentionally effortlessly? Do you like my little witticism I wrote below it? Do you like me?"

And we still take addictive tranquilizers to help with our insecurities—it's called distracting ourselves. In *Dopamine Nation*, addiction specialist Dr. Anna Lembke writes: "We're all running from pain. Some of us take pills. Some of us couch surf while binge-watching Netflix. Some of us read romance novels. We'll do almost anything to distract ourselves from ourselves. Yet all this trying to insulate ourselves from pain only seems to have made our pain worse."[6]

A much less obvious way we distract ourselves from the insecurities, challenges, and chaos of trying to be unique while at the same time fitting in, in the opinion of the existentialists, is by creating and attaching to fixed identities.

Bad Faith

In the late 1930s and '40s, when Dale Carnegie was in his heyday over here teaching Americans to develop impeccably winning personalities, Sartre was sitting in the middle of a café in Paris observing a waiter slip right into a plug-and-play identity.

Sartre noticed that this waiter, as he later described it in *Being and Nothingness*, seemed like he was doing a waiter impression. Sartre writes:

His movement is quick and forward, a little too precise, a little too rapid. He comes towards the customers with

a step a little too quick. He bends forward a little too
eagerly; his voice, his eyes express an interest a little too
solicitous for the order of the client . . . All his behaviour
seems to us a game. He applies himself to linking his
movements as if they were mechanisms, the one regulat-
ing the other; his gestures and even his voice seem to be
mechanisms; he gives himself the quickness and pitiless
rapidity of things. He is playing, he is amusing himself.
But what is he playing? We need not watch long before
we can explain it: he is playing *at being* a waiter in a
cafe.[7]

The waiter was doing exactly what Carnegie taught: playing a role, applying acting skills to his real life, feigning charm
and extroversion. I was a server once. The minute I got my little
uniform and my leather-bound notebook, I turned on an inner
waitress inside me that I didn't even know was there. I easily
performed the server archetype I'd watched my whole life. It
was like I was cast in a movie, and apparently, pretty gifted at
the part of "peppy waitress."

"Hi! I'm going to be taking care of you today. Can I start
you off with some drinks?" "Are you guys ready to order, or do
you need a few more min—no problem! I'll come back in a
few." "Oh yes, it's a very popular dish." "How's everything
tasting?" "Did you two save room for dessert?" "Of course,
there's always that little extra dessert pocket, tee-hee!" "Now,
there's absolutely no rush. I'm just going to leave the check
here; but again, no rush. I'll come back in a few."

Sartre would ask, Is this the way servers authentically talk
to their ophthalmologist? Is this how they walk, with this exaggerated, unnatural grace, through the mall? No. This is them
playing the part of a server. Just like people play the part of a

police officer, or wedding DJ, or flight attendant—who are known to take actual acting classes to perfect their role. While we would consider that doing a good job, Sartre would say that's living in "bad faith," when someone acts how they believe is expected of them, rather than in accordance with their true nature.

Bad faith is one of the most applicable and empathetic ideas of existentialism. Because Sartre understood the anxiety that comes from the burden of our freedom—and the idea that we're essentially nothing more than who we decide to be through our actions. He thought that we find ways to lessen our feeling of freedom by distracting ourselves with restraints. One type of restraint could be alarm clocks, which let us obey a brutal noise rather than face whether and when to get up on our own, and another kind of restraint is sliding ourselves into already created identities, such as a server. That's not to say any ol' server is a phony! Sartre just believed that if you're going to be a server, be yourself *as* a server. Like, don't buy your server costume at Party City—hand-make it. Metaphorically.

As you know, existentialists believe we distract ourselves from creating ourselves by glomming on to a fixed identity. Like muting our thoughts in *Gilmore Girls* reruns or misdirecting our existential angst into chipping a freshly painted nail, holding on to a fixed idea of our identity is cowardly and copping out as well.

Bad faith, another concept introduced by Sartre, is the opposite of authentic living. Bad faith is when we lie to ourselves to avoid freedom and responsibility. It's when we fail to accept the cards in our hand. Sartre noticed that some (read: many) people would rather adhere to societal norms than take control of their own freedom, so they delude themselves into believing they aren't free and blame their actions on unavoidable outside forces like societal rules, roles, or expectations. But it's easier to act like nothing can be changed than to face the reality of our chances.

What we're desperately trying to do when we proclaim "I am an aesthetician," or "I'm a runner," or "I'm a perfection-ist, clearly!" is give ourselves a structure in a world where no structure exists. Again, the existentialists would say this is un-derstandable, as they certainly empathized with how lost we can feel having a million different paths we could follow in life, and agreed that nobody wants to spend their lives stuck in a state of freedom-induced dizziness. But they say we're copping out (living with bad faith) if we just pick from the buffet of pre-made cultural roles.

In his podcast *Philosophize This!*, Stephen West[8] illustrates this point profoundly using a mime metaphor. How could you not love a mime metaphor? Imagine, he says, someone chooses the identity of a mime. Maybe they were born and raised in a family that talked way too much (his joke), so they yearned for a career of quiet. Miming becomes the premolded, socially rec-ognized role that makes them feel like a thing people can point to and name in this chaotic world, versus, say, a random, shape-less human being. This provides mimes with a lot of comfort—they don't need to think about what to do every day because they can easily just model themselves after the similar values, projects, and structure of other mimes. Claiming the identity of a mime also gives this person fulfillment and purpose: they feel significant evoking joy and side-eyes from strangers on the street.

And then, when the mime's life comes to a close, as Stephen says, "when people talk about [them] at [their] funeral . . . when all [their] mime friends are clocked out for the day and can ac-tually start talking, . . . they will always remember [them] as a mime. *He was a good mime! Salt-of-the-earth mime.*" This deceased mime is now part of a whole mime lineage. So in some small and silent way, their legacy lives on. Their time on earth was significant. It was worthwhile.

Nobody's poking fun at this. There's no shame in creating these roles to prevent ourselves from regularly freaking the fuck out. It's just that existentialists encourage us not to lose ourselves in our "mime" identity. Be a mime, but be *you* as a mime. And know that you off mime duty doesn't have to still be mime-like. Maybe when your white mime face and white mime gloves come off, you're the loudest one at the sports bar.

This is where the free-will part of existential thought comes into play. They call it *authenticity,* and in contrast to today's flavor of authenticity, which is a badge we claim when we intentionally reveal something truthful about ourselves, existentialism's authenticity is an action. Like self, authenticity is a verb. The process of authenticity is continually creating our essence in relation to others on their journey of creating themselves. Every moment contains possibilities for putting a narration to our situations.

Unlike with conventional authenticity, existentialists believed, it's natural to be continually altered by situations we're in and people we're around. We act differently depending on where we are. So it's actually more authentic, in existential-speak, to be changed by circumstances.

We contain a potpourri of selves. I used to think this was no bueno—that having more than one self meant you were a phony, conforming chameleon. But I now understand that's operating under the belief that there's a single static self hidden deep inside each of us waiting to be liberated, which is not the case. According to Storr, "Today's experts claim there is no authentic self." Just go back to your childhood home for

Thanksgiving and see if you don't revert back to drinking Smirnoff in water bottles buried under your bed to cope with your parents reverting back to treating you like you're of the age to have secret water bottles of Smirnoff buried under your bed. "Different versions of us emerge depending on where we are, what we're doing, who we're with and how aroused [I think he means excited] we happen to be," Storr says.

Self-help tells us that to be "aligned" we should add up to an authentic aesthetic, where all parts of each of us make sense. But an aesthetic is bad faith because you're not static. All aspects of you don't have to make logical sense. All of your pieces *not* fitting together like a puzzle is more authentic than their being in a perfect clean shape.

I'm always perplexed when I stroll through New York City during the holiday season and see bad faith sprawled out on the streets. For a few blocks by the behemoth Christmas tree in Rockefeller Center, fake Louis Vuitton belts, bags, and wallets are all laid out on the ground on bedsheets taking up half the sidewalk so passersby can barely pass, er, by without at least contemplating a purchase.

Over the jingles of Salvation Army volunteers soliciting coin donations and a mashup of tourists speaking in their native tongues, you can hear sounds of street sellers shouting, "That goes for fifty dollars, but for you, I charge forty-five!"

One year, I turned to Jesse and asked, "Do you think Louis Vuitton loses their minds over this?"

He replied by telling me that while studying abroad in Italy, he took a course on the business of fashion and learned that some luxury designer companies like Louis Vuitton actually allow it. Encourage it, even.

"By people going nuts for the replica products, it actually drives up the desire to get the real thing," he said. "People with the phonies bucket-list more for the real ones, crave the real ones, save for the real ones. The fake makes the authentic more valuable. Knockoffs make the real deal more desirable."

This is something the existentialists argued long ago. They relentlessly urged people to remain their authenticated version and not settle for a flimsy knockoff of themselves. The existentialists recognized that we've been conditioned to fit the mold, which is why they wrote tirelessly, in both their philosophical works and through metaphors in fiction, inspiring us to resist conformity. And then social media came along and taught us how to perfect the art of the knockoff.

The good news is, as with leather bags, the value for authenticity from others is way up. Sky high. Exorbitantly priced. *And* we're coming to know just how big a price we pay on an individual level for our own inauthenticity. Enter: suffering.

As Martha Beck writes, "Believing things that aren't true for us at the deepest level is the commonest way in which we lose our integrity. Then suffering arises—not as punishment, but as a signal that we're being torn apart. The purpose of suffering is to help us locate our internal divisions, reclaim our reality, and heal these inner rifts."[9]

This is exactly what happened to me.

I refer to my decade as a fiery public-facing health foodie as the time I spent wearing a "cantaloupe costume." I created a static self, a very specific personal brand, and it proved to be quite prosperous. I truly believed I was authentic for so thoughtfully and intentionally customizing myself, but now I realize that I did it within the parameters of our extrovert-celebrating, success-driven, follower-growing society.

When the incongruence between my inner and outer self had gotten far too painful, or as Dr. Maté says, my self became too fractured, I had to strip that cantaloupe costume off completely. As he explains in *The Myth of Normal*, conditions for disease can begin with a separation from the self, so it makes sense that one solution is to reintegrate our fractured parts.

Outside traditional psychotherapy, and working with a psychiatrist to test different medications, I self-designed a healing protocol that was a mashup of cult deprogramming, addiction recovery, and inspiration from people who had bravely reshaped their entire identities. This meant I anonymously zoomed into AA meetings, got deep into podcasts and documentaries about cults, and read, of course, Ricky Martin's memoir, *Me*.[10]

What do sobriety, deprogramming, and a sexy Latin pop star have in common?

1. Psychological pain, which Martha Beck says always "comes from internal splits between what your encultured mind believes and what feels deeply true to you"
2. Stunning feats of integrity repair and the end of self-betrayal

Ricky Martin's autobiography illuminates the struggles he faced in finding peace with his homosexual identity. Alcoholics Anonymous offers a path of healing through self-reflection, personal responsibility, and growth, while those unbrainwashed from a cult must grapple with the struggle of leaving an insular community and rediscovering autonomy. Every one of them delves into the perilous journey of individual metamorphosis.

Now obviously I am not a bon-bon shaking, leather-pants wearing, heartthrob superstar. But I am a person in a culture for whom there are expectations, parameters, norms. Ricky's stakes for coming out with an identity so opposite of what he'd displayed on stages for crowds as large as thirty thousand were arguably outwardly higher than mine—in that it could ruin his very public career (and piss off all those profiting off his fame). But inwardly, I imagine we were struggling from the same inner torture. One that an addict coming to terms with their fractured identity, or a cult member parsing what's really "them" and what's been implanted, also suffers from: a rebirth.

Of his journey of self-acceptance, Ricky writes: "I was going through a process of rebirth, and everything I did was done with the desire to wash away my secrets and anxieties so I could reconnect with the person I truly am."

In 2021, he told Trevor Noah on *The Daily Show* that many of those closest to him warned that coming out would end his career. "It was extremely painful for me until I said, 'I can't take it anymore. It's all about me now, it's not about what's happening outside. It's about what I need in order to be happy.'"[11]

Leaving a cult also takes immense courage. As Steven Hassan, licensed mental health counselor and cult expert, explains, "It requires questioning the beliefs and structures that have defined your life, and choosing to step into the unknown in pursuit of freedom and authenticity." As the poet E. E. Cummings once said, "It takes courage to grow up and become who you really are."

Ricky's road to healing and self-acceptance led him all across the world. On his trip to Egypt, a woman who had been eyeing him all day and couldn't hold her curiosity in any longer asked him, "Excuse me, sir, are you Ricky Martin?" He replied, "Yes, I am. But not the one you know."

I echo Ricky's sentiment there. On my road to healing and self-acceptance, which led me all across my house, from bed to living room to bed and sometimes the bathtub, I, too, became not the Talia people knew. I was dumbstruck to learn I'm not the bouncing, always-on, sociable, people-loving extrovert I thought I was, because that's who they saw. Once I took off my cantaloupe getup and stopped my fakery, I figured out I'm really a tender, contemplative, kinda-shy-at-first, people-observing introvert. I was terrified to let on about this extreme change in my behavior, so I called my friend in AA and talked about my fears about going back out into the world as someone who doesn't unconsciously pretend she's someone she's not. My friend explained that it was all about "reframing." She reframed weddings so they were no longer about getting shit-faced and now about celebrating a pair in love, which was helpful when she attended weddings after getting sober. I realized then that I had to reframe life so that it was no longer about performing a personality, but instead about living with integrity.

8

. . . .

Ineffable You

"The self is a story," Will Storr says in his epic book, *Selfie.* "One of the most critical functions of the human self is to make us feel in control of our lives. . . . Our brains invent stories . . . because they want to make us feel we're in control of our thoughts, feelings and behavior."

Another way to say that: so that every day in our life isn't just some random series of events from dawn to dusk. We each decide how to string our days together so that our existence can make at least a little cohesion as one big story. The self takes the confusing and conflicting aspects of our outer and inner worlds and creates a simpler story that aims to give us the comfort of control and security.

"We use stories to understand the world around us and what is happening in our own lives," writes psychology professor Gregory Berns in *The Self Delusion.*[1] "Your identity is the story that connects past-, present-, and future-yous."

I'm not saying we sit down with scissors, pictures, and a

blank book from a Michaels art supplies store and play with the snippets of our day until they tell a good story that we can rubber-cement in our scrapbook. *ALTHOUGH!* That's not *not* what we do every day when we sit down with our phone, an editing app, and a blank post on social media and play with snapshots of our day plus a genius caption until they tell a good story that we can post publicly on our feed and refresh nineteen times in the next hour to gauge our current self-worth based on the number of people who decided to tap their fingers twice on our story.

We also do this in our heads. It's called creating a narrative identity.

Coined by psychologist Dan P. McAdams, a "narrative identity"[2] is when we reflect on our past experiences to create stories that give our lives more significance. This can help us make better decisions. As Steve Jobs once said, "You can't connect the dots looking forward; you can only connect them looking backward. So you have to trust that the dots will somehow connect in your future."

It's remarkable how we each have our own perspective on our experiences. Emily Esfahani Smith, in *The Power of Meaning*,[3] suggests that a childhood experience like being thrown into the water by a parent to learn how to swim could explain someone's current attitude about taking risks and being a successful entrepreneur. Someone else could hate boats and not respect those in authority because of that water-dunking experience. A third person might leave that experience out of their life story entirely, seeing it as not meaningful or at all connected to who they are now. As McAdams puts it, "We are all the authors of our own stories and can choose to change the way we're telling them."

Berns argues that our sense of self comes not just from

memories but also from the meaning we give to the memories. And the problem is, not only are our memories wildly fallible, but the meaning we give to them is inextricably determined by the society we exist in. "If actions and beliefs define you," writes social psychologist Brian Lowery in *Selfless*, "it's only because they have social meaning." He continues, "If you give money to a person in need or a cause to help the downtrodden, are you a good person or a sucker? It's not that action per se that defines you, it's how the action is understood by others, and therefore by you."

Card Games

Whenever I'm feeling extra-existential, I play what I consider its theme song: "The Gambler" by Kenny Rogers. "The Gambler" is not just a song; it is a sermon. It tells you everything you need to know about life in only three and a half minutes. I have to paraphrase because I can't afford the copyright. It's the story of a presumably lonely man who meets another solo passenger on a train "bound for nowhere" (i.e., also on this destination-unknown journey we call life). The two lone travelers, likely out of pre-cell-phone boredom, decide to chat. The gentleman tells Kenny Rogers that he can see the melancholy on Kenny's face. Today, you can't even tell someone, empathetically, that you can see their lack of sleep on their face, so there's a reason this song is old, but I digress. The gentleman says that by the melancholic energy he senses from Kenny, Kenny must be out of aces—aces as in the cards in a fifty-two-card deck. The gentleman says he has a Spidey sense for reading people's hands by just looking at their eyes!

Then the gentleman tells Kenny that he'll give him free advice for some swigs of his whiskey, which is one helluva bribe, if you ask me. Kenny passes over his bottle because, I mean, how could he resist? It's like if a therapist came up to you in line at a bar and said, *Yikes, girl, I feel your miserable-wreck energy. Just gimme your martini, subscribe to my YouTube channel, and I'll tell you what to do.* And then she finishes your martini, plus the olive and the extra olive you ordered, and hits you with unsolicited advice.

After the whiskey has been swigged, the gentleman tells Kenny that he really needs to learn some (what I presume to be) basic poker strategy. He tells Ken that it's Gambling 101 to know what cards he ought to throw away versus which ones he should keep. *Self-awareness, baby, self-awareness.*

He emphasizes to Ken the importance of his knowing when to hold his cards, when to fold his cards, and when to toss them in a trash can with gas and a match and bolt away. The cards, of course, are individually meaningless. No card holds more value than another. The meaning one gives to a playing card is only in conjunction with other playing cards. This is what the gambler tells him is the secret of surviving life: being able to discern meaning by combining every single card in your hand. He tells Ken not to count his cash at the table, not just because money is filthy (literally!)—and unless you have a Wet Wipe it's really gross to touch coins and then bread—but also because he says there's plenty of time to count "when the dealing's done." This is a metaphor meaning "Don't waste your time on petty shit. Deal with that when you're dead, mmmk?"

Then he leans in and tells Kenny the biggest nugget: every hand can be a winner *and* every hand can be a loser. While Ken holds a blank stare, the gentleman reminds him that in life, we get only one hand to play. He seems to allude to the idea that life isn't about striving to find an ace stuffed in between train seats with strangers' lint and crumbs; rather, it's about accepting our cards and self-lovingly making the best of our reality. He tosses in a little reminder to Ken that nobody makes it out of life alive. "Don't take life too seriously," he seems to say. "The best that we can hope for is to die in our sleep."

These "cards," as the gambler calls them (and my dad, my entire life), are "facticity," which Sartre and Beauvoir wrote extensively about. Facticity, in existentialist jargon, is all about those unchangeable aspects of our existence that we can't do much about—like our looks, our family, and our knack for tripping over our own feet. Facticity is our nature and our nurture: our gender, age, nationality, sexual orientation, ethnicity, physical appearance, family background, socioeconomic status, innate health conditions, personal talents (or lack thereof). Possessing an uncanny ability to identify the perfect meme for any situation is facticity, as is being able to recite the entire dialogue of a favorite movie, word for word, or being intolerant of gluten—and people who chew too loud. Facticity is all those unchosen factors, or facts, of us. It's how the religious affiliation, geographic location, and shameful slight from our third-grade teacher Mrs. K infiltrated our psyche as a child. It's both our facticity *and* our freedom of choice that come together to create our life.

According to existentialists, we create our essence when we play our hand. It's pretty much the point of our lives.

But, Talia, if you believe the existentialists that the self is a creation, that it results from playing the hand you're dealt, then why do you hate so hard on the American ideal that comes from your frenemy Ben about being "self-made"?

The difference lies in the card game each person plays.

Existentialists say that our hand is our hand, that our facticity makes up the cards we hold, and while we can't reshuffle the deck, we can still decide how we play the game.

Benny Franklin and Co. believe we're playing Go Fish. They say that if we don't like our cards, we can just swap them out using hard work, focus, determination, and good ol' American grit.

Existentialists accept our cards. Cardwise, this means they want us to look closely at our collection of cards and craft one of the 2,598,960 possible unique five-card hands that can be built. They say, *Oh, you have the depression card? Good to know. What's that I see there by your pinky? The lower end of the six-figure salary? OK, we can deal with that. Do you have mommy problems? There's not even a card for that. It's presumed to be universal.* And then they encourage us to build whatever life we want from those cards.

Self-help guides call them limiting beliefs. They're the things they sell us tools to overcome. Any card that doesn't aid in our pursuits (of happiness, wealth, fame, etc.) should be thrown back in the pile immediately.

For me, I went thirty-two years not knowing that I was missing a card that was making my existence nearly impossible. When I finally found that dusty card, my depression/on-the-spectrum-of-bipolar card, I cherished the shit out of it. I finally understood how my hand made sense and how to play it to its best potential. This card is not a limiting belief that I can toss back in the pile and swap out for a stable, positive mood.

How to Be Ineffable

On the day of my first pregnancy ultrasound, a wave of nervousness rendered me motionless, standing in my closet, naked. I'm usually a decisive dresser, so this was new for me.

I looked to my left and saw my sweaters hanging from longest to shortest, because Marie Kondo said looking at lines that sloped up to the right made people feel more comfortable (unless that graph represents your debt over time). I looked to my right, where my shirts hung separately from my sweaters, because Marie Kondo also said that clothes were like kids in a high school cafeteria—more relaxed in the company of others who were very similar in type.

I bent to pull open my drawers, where my pants were horizontal in rainbow order, like a roll of Life Savers. My closet was curated for calm; I felt anything but.

WHAT DID A MOM WEAR?

Maybe I was afraid that if I looked *too* put-together, someone (a nurse? a doctor?) would conclude that I'd prioritize my appearance over my baby. Or if I showed up in sweats, they would add "Keep Child Protective Services on standby" to my file, assuming if I could barely take care of myself, my child would be screwed. So I forced jeans—lightly ripped but not so shredded to signal I would be taking my daughter to PG-13 movies before she was thirteen—over my swollen legs.

Next, I searched for a top. I was leaning toward black. I don't wear a lot of black, but it seemed like a safe bet. But when I reached for a black tee, I instantly thought of death, and even though I am only moderately superstitious, I couldn't risk it. But a colorful shirt might steal the nurse's thunder with her school-of-fish or Mickey Mouse scrubs. I love nurses, and I wanted them to shine.

So I pivoted toward something simple. Maybe a sweater with a giant duck on it, to show that I'd be a playful mom—or at least good at bath time? Or a turtleneck to show my child would answer the phone with a "May I ask who's calling?" if we still had a landline. No—a flannel. A flannel showed that I

would teach my child habits like remembering reusable shopping bags, flossing, and saying "No, thank you, Mrs. Sheldon"
on a playdate when offered a sugary snack.

Shoes were easy. Converse would prove I was a little classic
and a little edgy but still on the fence about breastfeeding in
public.

I rubbed tinted serum on my face and swiped on my least
dramatic mascara and a smear of blush on each cheek.

Dressed like the most mom-me I could be, I drove with
Jesse (who got ready in under five minutes) to the appointment.
In the tight, dark room, the tech swiveled her computer screen
thirty degrees and said, "There's your baby."

At that moment, with my carefully chosen clothes in a
messy pile on the floor, I became a mom. To this half-inch-long
child, I would be a mom, without having to craft the identity.

There is a practice in Tibetan Buddhism called the "Who
am I?" meditation. My aunt, a Tibetan Buddhist, demo'd it one
night over pasta and pinot. *Who am I? I'm a person who lives
in Berkeley. Who am I? I'm a seventy-eight-year-old—almost
seventy-nine-year-old—woman. Who am I? I'm a short
woman. Who am I? I'm sometimes embarrassed about what
my skin looks like. Who am I? I'm a psychotherapist. I'm a sister. I'm an aunt . . .*

The idea is that there's a self that lies beyond this thinking
self, beyond our self of identities. Underneath our profession,
occupation, appearance, wealth, or relationships to other people (facets of the "ego" in Buddhism) is a universal consciousness (our avocado pit, going back to that analogy). After we
name and visualize letting go of our material and immaterial
attachments, we can feel what is left. We can feel who we are
when nothing defines us.

This is the *ineffable self*. It's the "us" that's unspeakable:

there are no words to describe our nature, but there's *still* something inside us we can sense. As my aunt Barbara said, it's like holding a butterfly. If you close your hand tightly, you'll crush it. But if you float your hand out gracefully, you can give it a place calm enough to land.

Our ineffable self comes out in a flow state. Psychologist Mihaly Csikszentmihalyi came up with "flow" to describe a state of heightened concentration and satisfaction during an activity. It's when we feel so fully absorbed and deeply involved in what we're doing that the world around us blurs like a really high-def portrait-mode photo. It's less energetic than happiness, and it brings us a state of tranquility and fulfillment. It's also known as "optimal experience."

Ironically, we feel way more relaxed when we shelve our "selves" and defer to the flow. Flow is like being lost in a trance yet also completely present. It causes that overly opinionated narrator in our head to quiet down *for once.*

By seeking out activities that challenge and stretch our skills, setting clear goals, and focusing our attention on the present moment, we can cultivate flow experiences that bring us closer to living authentically. As Camus once said, "In order to understand the world, one has to turn away from it on occasion." Engaging in flow-inducing activities allows us to detach from the external distractions and expectations of the world, put down our "I am" identities for a bit, and just hang with our ineffable self.

"Maybe our deepest and most authentic happiness will be found only when we finally lay down this heavy burden of trying to be somebody," writes Lama Marut in *Be Nobody.* The "nobody" he tells us to "be" is the part of us that pops up when our "concentration is so intense that there is no attention left over to think about anything irrelevant or to worry about problems," as Csikszentmihalyi describes. That's what I call the ineffable self.

I've found that our ineffable self is usually a through line. You might be able to get in touch with it by going back to childhood. What were some attributes back in the day that made you the most you before you shushed your you to be more like everyone else? Like, I always noticed how unique it was that my best friend growing up was obsessed with detectives. She really jumped on the Harriet the Spy train, boasting that her name, Sloane the Spy, had a better ring to it. She was always toting around a notebook looking for clues, dusting for prints, spying on her family, which, once while peeping in her parents' room on February 14, resulted in mild PTSD. She followed the clues all the way to where she works now as a brilliant neuropsychologist, literally solving patients' brain mysteries so they can live better with their epilepsy.

I have also found that these ineffables are facets of ourselves that we think are universal but are not. Like in high school, I thought everyone hated math but loved English class. I genuinely thought math was some kind of universal torture that "they" imposed on us so that we didn't enjoy a full day of school *too* much. Even now, fourteen years out of high school, I find it hard to fully accept that there were kids whose butterflies came when the bell rang for rhombus and trapezoid o'clock, the way mine fluttered when it was time to pronoun-and-past-tense it up! Jesse sees the world through textures and textiles. He can remember a plate from a restaurant he ate at five years ago and the wall art from a hotel a decade ago. I don't see any of that because I'm busy eavesdropping on everyone around me. I love how author Glennon Doyle once said, "People who aren't writers don't constantly wonder if they're writers." Meaning: Come on. We *know* who we are.

Because why not, let's add a Japanese reference here. Ikigai is a gorgeous Japanese concept that translates to "a reason for being" or "a reason to wake up in the morning." It represents a sense of purpose, fulfillment, and a reason to live a meaningful life. The term *ikigai* is derived from the combination of *iki* (life) and *gai* (value or worth), and it suggests that true happiness and fulfillment come from finding the intersection of four fundamental elements: what you love, what you are good at, what the world needs, and what you can be rewarded for. When these four elements align, it is believed that individuals can experience a state of ikigai, in which they find a deep sense of meaning, fulfillment, and satisfaction in their lives—so pretty much what I am calling the ineffable self. Though I don't know of many Japanese existentialists, finding one's ikigai involves the same tools they recommend: introspection, self-reflection, and exploration of personal values and interests. It is a journey of self-discovery and understanding, aiming to align your actions and choices with your core values, passions, and strengths.

There's a famous story told by Rabbi Zusha (some know him as Reb Zushia) about a man who once visited him and asked, "Reb Zushia, when you die and get to heaven, aren't you afraid that you'll be asked why you weren't as great as Avraham Avinu or Moshe Rabeinu [presumably, stand-up guys with over 200K followers each]?"

"No," replied Reb Zushia. "I am more afraid that HaKadosh Baruch Hu [one of God's many monikers] will ask me, 'Why weren't you as great as Reb Zushia?'"

9

. . . .

The Sky

I'm lying outside in a lounge chair on a balmy summer night, looking up at the star-filled sky. Snug in my arms is my precious premature five-pound baby.

There was a time when I used to look up and feel completely inconsequential. I'd wail to Jesse, "If I died, nobody would even notice." While underneath thinking, *And nobody would care.* I applied that classic quandary about trees—"if a tree falls in a forest and no one is around to hear it, does it make a sound?"—but to *me* falling and it not making a dent.

That night, cuddling my perfect tiny Hannah, I found myself once again awash in the familiar feeling of insignificance, a feeling of just how minuscule I am compared with the billions of years the universe has existed before me and will continue to exist long after I'm gone. I looked down at the fresh new being in my arms and it hit me that the same is true for her: she, too, is also cosmically insignificant.

This is, I later learned, known as transcendence (a derivative of the word *transcend* that means "to exceed limitations"). A transcendent experience like this allows us to rise above the ordinary and connect with a higher reality, like the barriers between us and the wider world around us dissolve.

Psychologist William James (the same one from chapter 3 who coined the mind-cure movement back in the late nineteenth century) was also into transcendence. He described it as "a mystical experience."

I was breastfeeding, so I can assure you I wasn't on ayahuasca. Still, all I can say is that unlike my usual sense of dread that I'm a meaningless speck of nothingness, I all of a sudden felt like a blissful meaningless speck of nothingness!

This is how I know (in hindsight) I was "transcending," because in a transcendent state of mind, oddly, we experience a paradoxical state where we simultaneously feel connected and insignificant at the same time, all while being immersed in profound peace and serenity. Buddhists, who sometimes call this an "ego death," say it's when you lose your sense of self and become part of the universe. You release who your mind thinks you should be and embrace some true nature you feel inside. Whatever we call it, I can confirm it's delicious.

In a sense, the collective experience of the COVID-19 pandemic offered glimpses of transcendence and ego death, as it forced many of us to confront our own mortality and the fragility of human life. In the face of such a global crisis, we were reminded of our interconnectedness and shared vulnerability as a species; individuals around the world grappled with feelings of isolation, uncertainty, and existential dread. This collective experience prompted introspection and a reevaluation of priorities, leading some to experience moments of transcendence and ego death. (And no, I'm not going to call that a "silver lining" because I am not a toxic positivitist!)

But the big-kahuna epiphany I experienced that night was when I looked down at my daughter and just thought, *Nothing you do matters, sweetie.*

You're free, I thought. *I genuinely don't prefer whether you get a PhD in civil engineering and put blinking lights on every merge sign so I actually notice them, or if you decide to go to art school and then open a gingerbread-house museum, or if you choose to skip college altogether and become a fishmonger. There was no specific reason I birthed you, no mystical Purpose embedded in you that you must "find," lest you be a waste of space—or a waste of the thousands of dirty diapers to come.*

I remembered something I'd heard Neil deGrasse Tyson say. "There's been about 100 billion people who have ever lived," said deGrasse Tyson. "Do you know how many people can exist? You take a look at the genes, find how many combinations of genes can make an authentic human being, and it is a stupendously larger number than the hundred billion. What it means is, you are alive against stupendous odds. You are breathing air, observing sunsets, gazing into the night sky. Most people who could exist will never experience that. Because most people that could exist mathematically will never exist. So right there, you are as special a living entity as there ever was."

And I felt that. I felt that any way you do the arithmetic, Hannah was the most special living entity ever to be created.

But still. Nothing she does *matters* matters.

BECAUSE IT'S ALL MADE UP.

The value we place on things like goals, achievements, and

life's purpose is a human creation. The checklist of life "stuff" we get after being discharged from the maternity ward is just as arbitrary and subjective as Yelp reviews. It's like, *Congratulations, here's your bundle of joy. Oh, and by the way, here's your to-do list for the next eighty years.* But it's all made up! Sure, people say this restaurant's the bomb, but who decides that? Just like who decides what makes a successful life?

Sitting there with little Hanni wrapped snuggly in my arms, looking up at the vastness above, I realized that there is no ceiling on her life. The sky is really the limit. And not in a "reach for your dreams/you can be a WNBA-playing, stock-trading runway model–philanthropist–mother of three who grows and cooks her own food" kind of way. In a "there are absolutely no requirements hanging over your head" kind of way. As in FREEDOM. As in "Look, Ma—no rules!"

Of course, there are traffic laws and state mandates and a penalty for late library books, but otherwise there are no *actual* rules in life—no formal expectations.

And something just cracked open inside me. This time, instead of my recognition of my relative insignificance in the universe adding to my argument of the pointlessness of my continued existence, I was flooded with the feeling of freedom.

Because, I thought, *If there are no expectations for* her, *then there must not be expectations for* me. A sentiment echoed in my mind: *No one really cares what we're doing with our life. It's all made up.*

All that matters is what we choose to give meaning through our actions. I kissed the top of Hannah's tiny head and closed my eyes, holding her as tightly as I safely could.

When we come to accept that life is essentially a construct based on our own choices and values, the relief is almost orgasmic. In that sense, being reminded of our speck of significance is one helluva miracle, as it can help us give up the culturally created standards we've taken as fact. We can release the weight of an impractical notion of what defines a fulfilling life.

Liberating is an understatement. Once I flicked off culturally created definitions of a "life well spent," I was free to own my passion for the things that truly lit me up, even if they weren't stamped with society's seal of approval. I think in that moment I shed a burden heavier than all my baby weight. I was liberated. I realized I had in fact been walking around with societal values stuck to the bottom of my foot like toilet paper. I realized I had been holding myself accountable not only for goals that were beyond reach but for goals that weren't even critical to reach. Standards and expectations that actually meant jack shit to me.

This is the epitome of existentialism's "existence precedes essence."

Our baby exists before I, or they, know *who* they are. *What* their essence is. And they get to have fun figuring that out. And we get to feel joy watching them have fun figuring that out (while giving them snacks).

But as we've discussed ad nauseam, figuring that out causes nausea. Having free rein is an enormous obligation. It's exhausting to make even little decisions, like which delivery app to use to order what dish from what restaurant and how much to tip. Who's got it in them to *also* think about what values they want to live by?

Plugging Our Mortal Ears

I'm reminded of a story my acupuncturist told me about a time he miraculously healed a man from twenty years of chronic leg pain with one session of needling. Hours later, my acupuncturist closed up shop for the day and headed out. As he got to the parking lot, he saw the patient sitting in his car.

David asked him what he was still doing there so many hours later. The man replied, "I don't know what to do. I can't remember how to live without my pain." In a new way, maybe even more significant than the former, he was paralyzed all over again. This time, paralyzed by freedom.

This feeling of paralysis is the lack of feeling restricted in our choices. The thing is, even worse than having to bulk-write thank-you notes is having to choose what values you want to use to shape your life. Hence why, as the philosopher Iddo Landau noted in *Finding Meaning in an Imperfect World*, "many dedicate more thought in one evening to deliberating which restaurant or film they should go to than they do in their entire lifetime to deliberating what would make their lives more meaningful." I'm not sure I've ever heard a truer statement.

A therapist once told me, "Waking up with no plan is a certain kind of hell," when I'd shared with her my struggle to find any sort of daily rhythm as a new parent (and as a general person allergic to lame, stifling daily routines).

So to avoid that certain kind of hell—i.e., the existential angst and responsibility associated with the freedom of existence—we (individually and collectively as a society) come up with all sorts of distractions.

Ernest Becker, a Pulitzer Prize–winning philosopher, looked into this in his celebrated book *The Denial of Death*. In it, Becker explains the inconvenient irony that we humans can conceptualize our death while in the experience of living, which is but a more serious and pressing feeling of trying to enjoy a massage while knowing you will soon be forced to leave the table.

Becker believed that it's not the "leaving the table" we fear most—i.e., the actual moment of our death—but the *implica-*

tions of our passing: what our absence will say (or not say) about our life, what will be written in our eulogy, who will attend our funeral, what pastries will be served. "What man really fears is not so much extinction, but extinction with insignificance," he wrote.

To sort of plug our ears from the ringing of this fear of our insignificance, Becker said we create "immortality projects." He argued that our whole lives, in some respect, serve as immortality projects—ways we distract ourselves from our fear of complete impermanence and insignificance.

Creating and clinging to specific identities, soothing ourselves with things on screens or in headphones, rearranging our furniture, cleaning out our glove compartment, adding things to online shopping carts and then abandoning online shopping carts and then deleting "you abandoned your online shopping cart!" marketing emails. Getting shredded in the gym, getting crunk at the bar, getting high at a candy store—the ways we anesthetize ourselves vary across the board. But the one thing they share in common, these "immortality projects," is they divert our attention away from the reality: that in the grand scheme of things, we actually aren't immortal and eventually will be forgotten. "The idea of death, the fear of it, haunts the human animal like nothing else," he wrote. "It is a mainspring of human activity—activity designed largely to avoid the fatality of death, to overcome it by denying in some way that it is the final destiny of man."

Wondering where that pressure has its roots? Which founding father who is also on our $100 bill do you think wrote "If you would not be forgotten as soon as you are dead and rotten, either write things worth reading or do things worth the writing."

Eek. There's that existentialism nausea creeping in.

The thing is, the acknowledgment of this isn't what creates

our lunches coming back up our esophagus. It's the conflict between knowing this in our soul *and* getting relentless outside pressure to fight it.

Like it is with contentment, being ordinary is almost deemed a death sentence in our culture. Being OK with being ordinary sometimes goes so far as to be pathologized as depression. For so long, I thought there was something wrong with me for not wanting to achieve the stereotypical macro success all my peers were striving for. We're sold remedies to cure ordinary: supplements from the wellness industry, motivation from the self-help army, and productivity hacks from hustle culture. That's because we live in what I call a "meritocrazy" society— one that is crazily based on our merits and ranks our individual worth accordingly, pitting each of us against one another and pressuring us to work like crazy to outdo one another. I'm no mathematician, but I do know it's statistically impossible for all of us to be above average.

If you're sweating, me too. This is the shit that keeps Zoloft in business.

In a video by the School of Life,[1] they offer a startlingly paradoxical perspective of high achievers. They suggest flip-flopping that which denotes a significant life. While society often equates success with being exceptional, what if being able to lead a simple and fulfilling life, one of contentment and fulfillment in the ordinary, is the actual life of greatness?

"It seems odd to look at achievement through this lens, not as the thing the newspapers tell us it is," they say, "but—very often . . . those who put up the skyscrapers, write the bestselling books, perform onstage, or make partner may, in fact, be the unwell ones." Because those are the folks who feel compelled, at all costs, to be remarkable. The ones who may be high-achieving yet self-abusing.

What if we looked at the "ordinaries" as the privileged ones? Those unaffected by the pressure to be remarkable against impossible odds? The ones who can be self-accepting without being complacent?

In America, we're often teased for being this "supersize nation," in the sense that we feel a need to make our soda cups, cases of water, and breasts huge. We long for mansions, yachts, and cars that barely fit on one-way streets. But we also are a supersize nation in the sense of what we value. We value the big stuff. The loud stuff. The flashy stuff. The macro stuff. The stuff that makes us worth writing about. As Camus said, "You will never be happy if you continue to search for what happiness consists of. You will never live if you are looking for the meaning of life in extraordinary experiences."

Log on to Instagram and you'll see Ben's influence right there: every post is a celebration of something macro—a baby being born, a house being bought, a wedding being thrown, a milestone being applauded. Think about causes that warrant a family celebratory dinner: graduations, exam passings, baptisms, and bar mitzvahs. Go to a drugstore and see all the cards written to commemorate these macro milestones.

It's no wonder we're not taught to value the minutiae. No wonder we have a fear of triviality. It's said that sex sells, but so does significance. We perpetuate this phenomenon while we take part in it. It's a learned *and* practiced behavior. The things we see on social media are the big ones, so we come to believe that only big things belong on social media. (At least if we want to get big likes.) But I think this is one of those classic correlation, not causation, scenarios: the big things get the big likes because there are only big things to like.

I believe the fear of anonymity is all-consuming. To combat it, we strive for immortality. We're encouraged to leave a mark, an imprint, some indicator that WE WERE HERE, DAMMIT. We sit in our homes looking at photos of the upper echelon of celebrities freezing their handprints in the ground for all eternity with fear that nobody will give two shits about even a strand of our hair once we're long gone.

For most of my life, this fear of anonymity was my Achilles' heel. I've been completely obsessed with mattering ever since I can remember. Sometimes, diagnostic tools would tell me that this is my depression talking: that when I whisper some version of *I don't matter* to myself in my head, this is me presenting with common symptoms of depression—tied in with feeling a sense of worthlessness and low self-esteem.

True. But pondering one's mattering can also be just a common symptom of being human. Actually, it's exactly these introspective and existential quandaries that make us uniquely human, versus, say, a giraffe or a panda bear or a beetle.

This is why I love the existentialists. Because they tell me that pondering my existence, feeling distress, even acknowledging that, like, in the scheme of the world, I actually don't really play a huge role is kosher. It's healthy. It's OK. Which I find nine hundred times more therapeutic than a therapist or self-help guides or even my mom, who tells me, "Oh, come on, stop it. Of course you matter!"

YOU MAKE THE DIFFERENCE

One of my first jobs out of college was working as a page at *The Late Show with David Letterman*, where I put my valuable college degree to use by subwaying to Times Square every Tuesday to offer free (!!!!) live taping tickets (they were always free) to any tourists who could answer a Letterman trivia question

These questions ranged from "What nationality is Paul

Shaffer, the show's bandleader, eh?" to "In what episode did Letterman fire-extinguish Richard Simmons?" When I wasn't sharing a coworking space with the Naked Cowboy, I was in the theater's lobby, practicing the should-be-ancient art of "stanchioning." Not familiar? Stanchioning involves herding people through those vinyl lines that we often see at highly populated places like Disney World, airports, and hell. You know, where they corral you like cattle, except cattle get to roam around freely and you're trapped in a rope maze from which you can't escape. It's like you're either being tested on your ability to tolerate proximity to strangers or being judged for your pathetic conformity to weave a mile through an empty maze rather than having the courage to just tug the vinyl rope and crawl under.

At *The Late Show*, I also developed the equally, if not more important, life skill of talking at a crowd of people regretting many life decisions that had led them to that moment. Each day before a live taping, I would stand on a flimsy folding chair and recite a joke-filled ten-minute comedy set designed to break the ice for audience members and get them laughing out loud, since the show relied on audience laughter—not a fake laugh track. While the motive was to keep Dave's ego strong and let viewers at home hear how friggin' hilarious he was (which helped with the former), hiding sneakily in the underlying message of this pump-up speech was a very important life lesson that I make my husband live by today:

YOU CANNOT PEE UNTIL THE FIRST COMMERCIAL BREAK.

OK, one more:

YOU MAKE THE DIFFERENCE.

We'd say, and I quote: "OK, now I know at this point, you've all probably forgotten most of what I just said, but if you remember only one thing from the last ten minutes, let it be this: the more fun you have inside the theater, the more fun Dave will have, and in turn the better a show we'll produce. You make the difference."

Sure, it felt a little like a Smokey Bear campaign ("Only YOU can prevent wildfires") or a rally on recycling ("Only YOU can stop throwing soiled paper towels in the paper-recycling bin"), but it was empowering. And true. Dave didn't use a laugh track.

We *do* make a difference, each one of us *does* matter—but on a much smaller scale than we are taught to settle for. But that's what we're taught: that our lives are valued only if we have benches—metaphorical or made from wood in a park—named after us. But there isn't enough space for us each to have benches, so talk about a bullshit benchmark.

This false belief that we must break the fucking mold in order to be worth anything is incredibly destructive. I love how in Kane Brown's song "Famous Friends," he sings about his famous friends from his small town—like a teacher, a sheriff, a preacher, and a life-of-the-party football-star guy who is probably also the town's reigning champion of beer pong. Brown says that these "celebs" probably aren't known in the big city, but whatever. Where it matters, in their community, they're notable.

Unfortunately, this isn't the song that gets stuck in our head. Rather, it's the message that we *don't* matter, simply because what we see that matters is, as Jennifer Breheny Wallace writes in *Never Enough*, "unattainable at worst, and undesirable at best."

When societal expectations, which get upcycled into self-improvement propaganda, which turn into what's seen as Normal°, become impossible to ignore, we swallow them whole and come to depend on them as indicators of our self-worth. A genuine sense of mattering requires a sense of being seen and valued as an ineffable individual. Or you can just buy a plant.

A study conducted by psychology professor Ellen Langer at Harvard University[2] involved dividing nursing home residents into two groups. One group was provided with a houseplant to take care of, and the other group went without a plant. After a few months, researchers found that people who took care of the plant felt better in many ways than those who didn't have a plant.

Specifically, the residents who cared for the plant were more active and engaged, showed greater cognitive functioning, and reported higher levels of happiness and satisfaction. Remarkably, they lived longer than the ones without a plant.

This study shows how doing meaningful things, even small tasks like taking care of a plant, can help us feel purposeful and connected, and also improve our well-being and lifespan.

I once heard the saying "The macro is made of the micro."

Though popularized as a hustle-culture mantra (as in, consistently doing the micro-actions will create macro results), I've taken it to mean that our macro life is made of micro-moments. Like some people excel with nearsightedness and others with farsightedness (and I still don't comprehend the difference), I have always looked at life close-up, and I have felt at odds with a world so focused on the macro. I tried hard to hop aboard the macro train, giving importance, energy, and priority to the BIG THINGS that I see valued OUT THERE. The BIG THINGS that warranted a prize, an email blast to extended family, or a celebratory dinner at Dakota's Steakhouse (RIP).

So I tried to derive meaning from what I saw around me: good grades, noteworthy achievements, career success, and public accolades. But through that, I found it was the in-between things (the micro) that gave macro meaning to my days—a quick joke shared with a shy stranger, a shirt found on sale at the Gap that brought out my eyes, a free coffee when you filled up a frequent-buyer card.

With each passing year, I felt more like a depressed alien, afraid that the way I found meaning in life might never make sense to other humans. I told myself repeatedly: *Be happier—you have a book deal. You have a K in your follower count. You have a lovely home. A hot husband—and an even hotter dog. You were on* Good Morning America, *woman!* It didn't work, though. So I thought something was wrong with me. What else could explain why having dreams I'd seen on others' vision boards made me feel the same level of arousal as I get on a good-hair day?!

But then came Hannah. Once she was the size of a mere sesame seed, I suddenly found myself somewhere I'd never known existed. I met doctors and nurses who thoughtfully obsessed about inches in a sonogram, I read millions of women discussing hassles like heartburn and hair loss on message boards, and I saw strangers on social media celebrating my belly growing from the size of a grape to a cantaloupe.

Apparently, there had always been this underworld of folks who, like me, derive as much joy from seeing their baby lift their head a centimeter off the ground in tummy time as I'd seen others experience from seeing their face projected on the big screen in Times Square.

I had just missed it because I was stuck on the surface, where my attention was so impressively being hijacked by the LOUD things in our culture, like money, career success, and how our hat looks in our beach vacation photo needed to grow one's #PersonalBrand.

See, it's the macro that makes the media, but it's the micro that makes a life. That's why, even though putting on a duvet cover is easier than dressing baby Hannah, doing so has filled me with contentment.

I've always favored mini-interactions. Those seemingly benign quickies with strangers leave you with the most pleasant taste in your mouth. It's thrilling that research is coming out to back up this delight. Researchers call these "weak ties": relations with someone we know only in passing. People with a lot of weak ties generally felt much happier, especially on days with a low number of interactions, like if you work from home and venture out only to the dog park or for a pizza slice. Unfortunately, we don't post photos of our weak-tie interactions, so we don't get reminders to seek or cherish them. There sure is evidence of strong ties, though, like group pics of sixteen girls in matching tied bikini bottoms on a boat, or six couples, with the men in ties at a wedding. But proof of a delightful chitchat with your barista sadly doesn't make the 'gram. Neither did the time I was asked by a stranger at FedEx to sign her prenup, or when a Lululemon salesperson learned I was pregnant before my family.

In *The Power of Strangers*, Joe Keohane explains that these commonplace interactions feel so good because we're designed to have them. "If our distant ancestors killed every stranger they met, we wouldn't have made it very far as a species," he writes.[3]

When we first got our Jeep Wrangler, Jesse and I would drive around town and notice some other drivers giving us what looked like a little greeting. "I think all Jeep owners wave to one another!" I shouted to Jesse as I started waving back like I was seeing an old friend across the street. Nothing lights my fire as much as an unplanned human connection. It wasn't until we saw enough casual two-handed Vs propped on steering wheels that it dawned on me that *that* might be the move, not an enthusiastic mom wave that rightfully got ignored.

I became obsessed with this secret handshake of sorts, making sure never to miss a Wrangler, lest I commit the crime of leaving someone hanging. Jesse, when driving, was less alert to the cars passing, so I started yelling, "JEEP," from the passenger seat so he'd know to do it, too. Sometimes the driver wouldn't Jeep-wave back, and then I'd feel embarrassed, like when you're in a restaurant and someone waves to you and you wave back, but actually they're waving to someone behind you, so you want to disappear into your plate of mashed potatoes. But even though I sometimes felt dejected, it was worth the risk, because every time a stranger and I Jeep-waved at each other, I felt electricity zip through my body. Connection. Brother, er, sister, er, peoplehood. Camaraderie. I knew nothing of the other driver, yet we shared something in common, and that felt warm and cozy, the way that encountering another American on a foreign vacation feels like you just ran into a cousin.

It's kind of reverse "don't sweat the small stuff" thinking (the title of a bestselling book). While meant to be a motto for not letting mixing your whites and darks in the washing machine ruin your week, the opposite is *to* let a simple Jeep wave make yours. Let a smile shared with a stranger feel significant.

Using this logic, we can see how even the ordinary can feel like a gift. In *The Power of Meaning*, Emily Esfahani Smith[4] mentions the idea of "high-quality connections," which comes from organizational psychologist Jane Dutton. Dutton studies the impact these small, high-quality connections can have on people in the workplace. Her research confirmed what you probably know in your heart to be true: the most common way people feel devalued is by being ignored. Dutton did a deep dive into a large hospital janitorial staff and found that something as simple as eye contact from a doctor, or a "good morning" from a patient, could turn a janitor's day from feeling meaning-less to valuable. It's incredible. It's beautiful. We saw this dur-ing the coronavirus pandemic when grocery store employees and teachers (rightfully) got recognition as our heroes. Smith writes: "Feeling like part of the group can make even the most mundane tasks seem valuable and worth doing well. . . . Brief interactions can be demeaning—but they can also be digni-fying."

But embracing the ordinary is radical in this world, which means it paradoxically requires great courage. As J. D. Salinger writes in *Franny and Zooey*, "I'm sick of not having the cour-age to be an absolute nobody."

Life is a wild mix of contradictions and chaos. Like an old-timey medicine show, it's a stage where promises of miraculous cures are peddled alongside sketchy side effects lurking just be-neath the surface. Society overwhelms us with guidelines for success, dictating how we should live and what will bring us happiness, similar to those snake-oil salesmen who once mes-merized crowds with their magic cure-all remedies.

Yet, beyond the glittering I lies a somber truth: the burden of deciphering reality from illusion falls squarely upon our shoulders. In the grand theater of existence, where narratives of achievement and fulfillment are relentlessly sold to us, it's easy to lose sight of our authentic selves amid the clamor of societal expectations. We're left grappling with questions of identity, purpose, and meaning.

When you hear "snake oil," you think of phony cures sold by dishonest sellers trying to make a quick buck. But in the modern era, could we broaden our understanding to encompass the myriad messages and products that contradict our very humanity? Whether it's the ceaseless race for material possessions or the unending search for social media validation, we're constantly bombarded with narratives that jeopardize our sense of self and that distance us from our fundamental human nature.

Amid this existential maze, the only way out is inside. If we stay skeptical and think critically, we can see through the lies and take control of our lives.

Trust me, nobody's as surprised as I am that what has helped me climb out of crippling self-hatred the most was history. But understanding that the reason I wound up in a place following some bogus and incredibly harmful (like, life-threateningly harmful) ideas is because of historic forces still at play in our present has single-handedly changed my life.

We have to be careful not to make our life itself a performance, an event for which there is no real purpose. We've all been to events where there was no actual event other than getting dressed up and taking photos to be able to show everyone you went to the event. The entire event is taking pictures of the event. Without critical thinking, our lives can be that way, too. Our whole life can be just performing life. Playing dress-up.

True fulfillment lies not in the applause of others but in the quiet moments of self-reflection and introspection when we confront the fundamental truths of our existence.

So, I still lie in bed afraid of feeling insignificant. But now I realize that I'm not abnormal—I'm human.

Epilogue: Claps

I hastily devour a slice of vegan banana bread while balancing a paper cup filled with lukewarm rooibos with my two free fingers. It's a Tuesday morning in a small library biography room.

"All right, ladies!" the librarian whisper-shouts. "If everyone could please make their way to their spot, I'd love to start."

With all the grace of a circus act, we maneuver our way to designated spots, attempting to gracefully lower ourselves onto yoga mats, mindful of our postpartum ailments. It's a delicate dance of avoiding our healing vaginal tears, C-section stitches, and leaking bloated breasts, all while keeping our precious bundles of joy intact.

Under the gentle guidance of Adrianne, our sagelike leader, we embark on a journey of truth sharing and emotional release. From husbands unwilling to touch a diaper to the existential dread of returning to the corporate abyss, our confessions range from the mundane to the borderline absurd. Some moms grapple with the challenges of breastfeeding, while others struggle with the challenges of mothers-in-law. One brave soul even admits to contemplating punt-kicking her overly enthusiastic dog out of sheer desperation.

As the session approaches its conclusion and the first signs of infant restlessness emerge, Adrianne suggests leading us in a few goodbye songs.

"If you're . . ." she begins.

I scan the room, witnessing the sea of strained expressions rearrange into smiles, as if the tune were a spell.

"Happy and you know it clap your hands!" she continues with glee.

Instinctively, moms join their little ones' tiny hands and smooth them together to create a symphony of muted baby claps. The irony isn't lost on me. Here we are, a group of exhausted, emotionally frazzled moms, desperately trying to find happiness in the chaos of motherhood, all while singing a children's song like it's the key to unlocking the secrets of the universe.

I wonder how many moms are feeling happy. I wonder how many moms are feeling the disconnect. I'm curious how they've shoved, displaced, minimized, or whatever'ed their pain. I wonder if they feel the reverberations of their current truth against the contrast of the song's meaning.

I wonder if they're beating themselves up. I wonder if they're thinking, *I know I should feel happier*, while they stomp their feet and shout "Hooray!" I wonder if they're scared that they're broken in some way. That they aren't normal.

The disconnect between the idealized notion of happiness portrayed in the song and the stark realities of our lives is palpable, hanging in the air like the scent of freshly baked banana bread.

In an attempt to distract myself from going deeper into the

existential bowels of my mind, I look around the room. I notice an old library book facing out on a shelf just behind Adrianne and her smile. The cover reads, *The Autobiography*, in an old-timey print under an old-timey photo. *The Autobiography of Benjamin Franklin.*

Amid the chorus of muted baby claps, I can't help wondering if Benjamin Franklin himself would chuckle at the absurdity of it all. "The constitution only guarantees the American people the right to pursue happiness," I can hear him say, as Camus finishes his sentence with "And . . . what is happiness but the simple harmony between a [person] and the life [they] lead?"

Clap clap.

Acknowledgments

This book was a solo odyssey—and a helluva taxing one at that. While many book acknowledgments vouch that "it takes a village," my village people were less about helping with the words on the page and more about keeping me sane enough to actually write them. In a sense, working on this book made me feel like a racecar driver, whirling around like a lunatic, convinced that if I just kept going, I'd eventually cross some kind of finish line. Without my world-class, much-beloved pit crew, I'd undoubtedly still be out there, driving in circles—or broken down somewhere, out of gas. But after what . . . five years? I've finally parked the car. And for that, I'm eternally grateful and endlessly indebted to:

Nina Shield, who gifted me the opportunity of a lifetime to write this book. You are a dream-maker, my friend. x2!

Lauren Appleton, who swooped in and embraced this project like the best of adopted mothers. So lucky we became a team.

Michele Martin, the most patient of agents. Thank you for your lack of pressure and abundance of support!

Ashley Alliano, for cheerfully dealing with deadlines and details that make me need Tums.

My anonymous copy editor (CE), without whom danglers, redundancies, and maybe even copyright infractions would abound! Your last query is framed on my desk.

Leigh Stein, for helping me unscramble my brain and embrace my love for Ben.

Ms. Rachel, for free childcare and catchy background music.

Micki Rosenthal, for tolerating my weekly laments about the highs and lows of writing this book for, what, over three years?

United Oxford Health Insurance, for covering that ^ with only a $15 co-pay.

Jackie Mahoney (shout out to Flex + Flow Bodywork!), for loving on my nervous system and my soul.

Miranda Anderson, for friendship, inspiration, and the most snuggly spaces to write, rewrite, procrastinate, and re-rewrite.

Aunt Barbara, for wisdom over breakfasts and support at all hours.

Alexis, for the title assist! And the deep talks and real cheerleading.

Nin, you needed *Party in Your Plants*, but you model nonconformity. I love you, baby sis.

Sloane, my #1 pit crew member for three decades. I'd be lost without you.

Mom, for the thoughtful edits, and Dad, for the curious thoughts.

Jesse, for refusing to let me quit every time I declared (!!!!!) that I would. For picking up the childcare when Ms. Rachel couldn't. And for everything, always. I love you more than words.

ChatGPT, for helpful synonyms and kind remarks on my "interesting connections between ideas"! Somehow you know my love language is words of affirmation, and it is very much appreciated.

Hannah, you are my meaning muse.

And for family, friends, and strangers, for letting me voice record at will.

Notes

Chapter 1: Normal°

1. Naoki Higashida, *The Reason I Jump: The Inner Voice of a Thirteen-Year-Old Boy with Autism*, trans. K. A. Yoshida and David Mitchell (New York: Random House, 2013).
2. Jonathan D. Schaefer, Avshalom Caspi, Daniel W. Belsky, et al., "Enduring Mental Health: Prevalence and Prediction," *Journal of Abnormal Psychology* 120, no. 2 (February 17, 2016), https://doi:10.1037/abn0000232.
3. Tami Simon, "Gabor Maté: A Personal View of Healing into Wholeness in a Toxic Culture," *Sounds True*, December 20, 2022, https://resources.soundstrue.com/transcript/a-personal-view-of-healing-into-wholeness-in-a-toxic-culture/.
4. Gordon Marino, *The Existentialist's Survival Guide: How to Live Authentically in an Inauthentic Age* (New York: Harper Perennial, 2018).

Chapter 2: Divine ~~Intervention~~ Indoctrination

1. The Holy Bible, King James Version, Ecclesiastes 9:11.
2. Friedrich Nietzsche, *Twilight of the Idols*, in *The Portable Nietzsche*, edited and translated by Walter Kaufmann (New York: Viking Penguin, 1954), 493.

3. David McRaney, *You Are Not So Smart: Why You Have Too Many Friends on Facebook, Why Your Memory Is Mostly Fiction, and 46 Other Ways You're Deluding Yourself* (New York: Gotham Books, 2011).
4. Albert Camus, *The Rebel* (New York: Vintage Books, 1991), 22.
5. Amanda Montell, *Cultish: The Language of Fanaticism* (New York: Harper Wave, 2021).
6. Robert Jay Lifton, *Thought Reform and the Psychology of Totalism: A Study of "Brainwashing" in China* (New York: Norton, 1961).
7. Johann Hari, *Lost Connections: Uncovering the Real Causes of Depression—and the Unexpected Solutions* (New York: Bloomsbury USA, 2018).

Chapter 3: Flexing Mind Muscles

1. Beth Blum interviewed by Zachary Davis, *Writ Large* podcast, October 6, 2020.
2. Will Storr, *Selfie: How We Became So Self-Obsessed and What It's Doing to Us* (New York: Overlook Press, 2017).
3. Steve Shipside, *Samuel Smiles' Self-Help: A 52 Brilliant Ideas Interpretation* (London: Infinite Ideas Limited, 2008).
4. Barbara Ehrenreich, *Bright-Sided: How the Relentless Promotion of Positive Thinking Has Undermined America* (New York: Metropolitan Books, 2009).
5. Storr, *Selfie*.
6. Ehrenreich, *Bright-Sided*.
7. William James, *The Varieties of Religious Experience: A Study in Human Nature* (New York: Longmans, Green, 1902).
8. Rhonda Byrne, *The Secret* (New York: Atria Books/Beyond Words, 2006).
9. Rhonda Byrne, *The Secret* (Atria Books/Beyond Words, 2006), DVD.

Chapter 4: All About the Benjamin (Franklin)

1. Jess McHugh, *Americanon: An Unexpected U.S. History in Thirteen Bestselling Books* (New York: Dutton, 2021).
2. Darrin M. McMahon, *Happiness: A History* (New York: Grove Press, 2006).
3. Benjamin Franklin, *Poor Richard's Almanack*, edited by Richard Saunders (Philadelphia: Printed and sold by B. Franklin, 1732).

4. Arthur C. Brooks, "The Happiness Advice of Ben Franklin," *The Atlantic*, May 2022, https://www.theatlantic.com/family/archive /2022/05/ben-franklin-happiness-self-improvement-advice /629767/.

5. Walter Isaacson, *Benjamin Franklin: An American Life* (New York: Simon & Schuster, 2003).

6. Brooks, "The Happiness Advice of Ben Franklin."

7. Franklin, *Poor Richard's Almanack*.

Chapter 5: If You're Eudaimonic and You Know It, Clap Your Hands

1. Martin Seligman, *Authentic Happiness: Using the New Positive Psychology to Realize Your Potential for Lasting Fulfillment* (New York: Free Press, 2002).

2. Ruth Whippman, *America the Anxious* (New York: St. Martin's Press, 2016).

3. Svend Brinkmann, *Stand Firm: Resisting the Self-Improvement Craze* (Cambridge: Polity Press, 2017).

4. Susan David, *Emotional Agility: Get Unstuck, Embrace Change, and Thrive in Work and Life* (New York: Avery, 2016), 54.

5. Fyodor Dostoevsky, *Winter Notes on Summer Impressions*, translated by Kyril FitzLyon (New York: New Directions, 1955).

6. Daniel Wegner, *White Bears and Other Unwanted Thoughts* (Cambridge, MA: MIT Press, 1989).

7. NPR, "President Obama Is Familiar with Finland's Heavy Metal Scene. Are You?," *NPR*, May 17, 2016, https://www.npr.org/2016 /05/17/478409307/president-obama-is-familiar-with-finlands -heavy-metal-scene-are-you.

8. Mahmudul Islam, "Why Finns Have an Affinity with Metal Music," *Nomad Today*, September 20, 2019, https://www.thenomadtoday .com/opinion/mahmudul-islam/why-finns-have-an-affinity-with -metal-music/20190920151949002961.html.

9. Barbara Held, *Stop Smiling, Start Kvetching* (New York: St. Martin's Griffin, 2001).

10. Alice Feeney, *I Know Who You Are* (London: HQ, 2019).

11. Tim Lomas, *Happiness—Found in Translation: A Glossary of Joy from Around the World* (Long Island City, NY: The Experiment, 2019).

12. Bronnie Ware, *The Top Five Regrets of the Dying: A Life Transformed by the Dearly Departing* (Carlsbad, CA: Hay House, 2012).

13. Albert Camus, *Nuptials,* 1938.

14. Simone de Beauvoir, *The Ethics of Ambiguity,* translated by Bernard Frechtman (Secaucus, NJ: Citadel Press, 1948).

15. Arthur C. Brooks, *From Strength to Strength: Finding Success, Happiness, and Deep Purpose in the Second Half of Life* (New York: Portfolio, 2022), 10.

16. Adam Grant, "There's a Name for the Blah You're Feeling: It's Called Languishing," *The New York Times,* April 19, 2021, https://www.nytimes.com/2021/04/19/well/mind/covid-mental-health-languishing.html.

17. Martin E. P. Seligman, *Flourish: A Visionary New Understanding of Happiness and Well-Being* (New York: Free Press, 2011).

18. Elise Loehnen, "Oliver Burkeman: The Fallacy of Time Management," *Pulling the Thread,* https://www.eliseloehnen.com/episodes/oliver-burkeman-the-fallacy-of-time-management.

Chapter 6: Satisfaction Guaranteed

1. Barry Schwartz, *The Paradox of Choice: Why More Is Less* (New York: Ecco, 2004).

2. Mark Manson, *The Subtle Art of Not Giving a F*ck: A Counterintuitive Approach to Living a Good Life* (New York: HarperOne, 2016).

3. Sarah Knight, *The Life-Changing Magic of Not Giving a F*ck: How to Stop Spending Time You Don't Have with People You Don't Like Doing Things You Don't Want to Do* (New York: Little, Brown and Company, 2015).

4. Frank Martela, *A Wonderful Life: Insights on Finding a Meaningful Existence* (New York: Harper, 2020).

5. Russ Harris, "A Values-Based Approach for the New Year and Beyond," Anxiety and Depression Association of America, accessed September 1, 2024, https://adaa.org/learn-from-us/from-the-experts/blog-posts/consumer-professional/values-based-approach-new-year-and.

6. Oliver Burkeman, *Four Thousand Weeks: Time Management for Mortals* (New York: Farrar, Straus and Giroux, 2021).

7. Pew Research Center, "About Three-in-Ten U.S. Adults Are Now Religiously Unaffiliated," December 14, 2021, accessed September 1, 2024, https://www.pewresearch.org/religion/2021/12/14/about-three-in-ten-u-s-adults-are-now-religiously-unaffiliated/.

8. Dan Rookwood, "Dad Jokes with Mr Jerry Seinfeld," *Mr Porter,* June 7, 2017. https://www.mrporter.com/en-us/journal/lifestyle/dad -jokes-with-mr-jerry-seinfeld-352340.

9. Richard H. Thaler, "The Coin Toss Decision Study," *Journal of Behavioral Economics* 12, no. 4 (2005): 45–58.

10. Nancy Groves, "EL Doctorow in quotes: 15 of his best," *The Guardian,* July 21, 2015, https://www.theguardian.com/books/2015/jul /22/el-doctorow-in-quotes-15-of-his-best.

11. Timothy D. Wilson and A. T. Norton, "People Would Rather Be Electrically Shocked Than Left Alone with Their Thoughts," *Science,* July 23, 2014, accessed September 1, 2024, https://www.sci ence.org/content/article/people-would-rather-be-electrically-shoc ked-left-alone-their-thoughts.

12. Bill Burr, *You People Are All the Same,* directed by Jaime Eliezer Karas (New York: Netflix, 2012).

13. Friedrich Nietzsche, *Nietzsche: Untimely Meditations* (Cambridge University Press, 1997).

Chapter 7: Self Is a Verb

1. Gish Jen, "Philosophies of Self: East-West Distinctions," *Big Think,* last modified July 12, 2023, https://bigthink.com/the-well/philo sophies-of-self/.

2. Thomas Sowell, *The Thomas Sowell Reader* (New York: Basic Books, 2011).

3. Gabor Maté, *When the Body Says No: Understanding the Stress-Disease Connection* (New York: Wiley, 2003).

4. Susan Cain, *Quiet: The Power of Introverts in a World That Can't Stop Talking* (New York: Crown, 2012).

5. Will Storr, *Selfie: How We Became So Self-Obsessed and What It's Doing to Us* (New York: Overlook Press, 2018).

6. Anna Lembke, *Dopamine Nation: Finding Balance in the Age of Indulgence* (New York: Dutton, 2021).

7. Jean-Paul Sartre, *Being and Nothingness: An Essay on Phenomenological Ontology,* trans. Hazel E. Barnes (New York: Philosophical Library, 1956) [originally published in French in 1943].

8. Stephen West, "Episode 93: Existentialism; The Essence of Existentialism," *Philosophize This!,* podcast, last modified January 25, 2016, https://www.philosophizethis.org/transcript/episode-162-tran script.

9. Martha Beck, *The Way of Integrity: Finding the Path to Your True Self* (New York: Penguin Life, 2021).
10. Ricky Martin, *Me* (New York: Crown, 2010).
11. Kevin Sullivan, "Ricky Martin Says Coming Out as Gay Was 'Extremely Painful' but 'Important' for His Career," *People*, March 26, 2023, accessed September 1, 2024, https://people.com/music /ricky-martin-coming-out-gay-extremely-painful/.

Chapter 8: Ineffable You

1. Gregory Berns, *The Self Delusion: The New Neuroscience of How We Invent—and Reinvent—Our Identities* (New York: Basic Books, 2022).
2. Dan P. McAdams, *The Stories We Live By: Personal Myths and the Making of the Self* (New York: Guilford Press, 1993).
3. Emily Esfahani Smith, *The Power of Meaning: Crafting a Life That Matters* (New York: Crown, 2017).

Chapter 9: The Sky

1. *The School of Life,* "Overcoming the Need to Be Exceptional," accessed July 19, 2024, https://www.theschooloflife.com/article/over coming-the-need-to-be-exceptional/.
2. Ellen J. Langer, "The Illusion of Control," *Journal of Personality and Social Psychology* 32, no. 2 (1975): 311–28.
3. Joe Keohane, *The Power of Strangers: The Benefits of Connecting in a Suspicious World* (New York: Random House, 2021).
4. Emily Esfahani Smith, *The Power of Meaning: Crafting a Life That Matters* (New York: Crown, 2017).

About the Author

Talia Pollock is a writer, speaker, mother, and armchair philosopher who infuses humor into wellness discussions to navigate life's complexities.

Her debut book and podcast, *Party in Your Plants*, promoted light-hearted, healthy living and non-miserable, plant-based eating. This book and supplemental Substack newsletter, Existennial, modernize existentialism to free us from the pressures of relentless self-improvement.

Talia's work has been shared on platforms like *Good Morning America*, *People* magazine, *The Dr. Oz Show*, *Mindbodygreen*, *Bustle*, *Runner's World*, and her small-town's local paper next to breaking news of a bear sighting. In a previous life, she performed stand-up comedy on stages throughout NYC, and in her current life, Talia writes, talks too deeply with strangers, and lives with her two daughters and one husband in Brooklyn.